SCOTT FORESMAN ENGLISH

IN CONTACT 1

BEGINNING

Second Edition

Barbara R. Denman
Prince George's County Adult Education Program
Prince George's County, Maryland

In Contact 1, Second Edition

Pearson Education, 10 Bank Street, White Plains, NY 10606

Editorial directors: Allen Ascher and Louise Jennewine
Acquisitions editor: Bill Preston
Director of design and production: Rhea Banker
Development editors: Barbara Barysh and Laura Le Dréan
Production manager: Alana Zdinak
Production supervisor: Liza Pleva
Managing editor: Linda Moser
Senior production editor: Virginia Bernard
Senior manufacturing manager: Patrice Fraccio
Manufacturing supervisor: Edith Pullman
Photo research: Quarasan and Aerin Csigay
Cover design: Charles Yuen
Text design and composition: Quarasan
Photo and illustration credits: See p. vi.

Library of Congress Cataloging-in-Publication Data
Denman, Barbara R.
    In contact 1: beginning / Barbara R. Denman.—2nd ed.
        p. cm.—(Scott Foresman English)
    Includes index.
    ISBN 0-201-57979-0
    1. English language textbooks for foreign speakers. I. Title.
II. Series.

                                                                99-33872
PE1128.D376   1999   CIP
428.2'4—dc21

10 11 12 13 14 15-WC-10 09 08 07

CONTENTS

SUMMARY OF SKILLS

CREDITS

Illustrations: Robin Brickman pp. 22, 43, 43, 45, 51; Tom Brocker/Precision Graphics p. 91; Chris Celusniak p. 33; Renee Daily p. 97 (b); Julie Durrell p. 23 (k. & l.); Felipe Galindo pp. 18, 26; T. R. Garcia p. 47 (t); Patrick Girouard pp. vii, viii, ix (1.–5., 7.–16), 14 (t), 15, 37,42, 70, 75, 76, 77, 78, 88, 110; Dan Grant pp. 49 (b), 51 (bl), 101, 113 (m); Al Hering pp. 11, 14 (m), 86; Tim Jones pp. 28, 60, 63 (b), 67 (b), 122, 125, 126; Brian Karas pp. 19, 23 (a.–j.), 87; Kees de Kiefte pp. 12, 16, 17, 20, 47 (m & b), 53; Judy Love p. 21; Katherine Mahoney pp. 2, 65, 66, 67 (t), 73, 85, 98; Bob Marstall p. 82; Matt Mellit pp. 83, 84 (t); Jan Palmer pp. 71, 117, 118; Bill Peterson pp. x, ix (6.), 13, 25, 44 (m & b), 102; Rolin Graphics pp. 109, 124; Philip Scheuer pp. 1, 3, 4, 6, 9; Steve Schindler pp. 34, 54, 55 (t), 58, 59, 61, 108; Carol Schweigert p. 29; Randy Verougstraete p. 121.

Photos: p. 7, (tl) Coris/Wally McNamee, (tc) Reuters/Rose Prouser/Archive Photos, (tr) Reuters/Ted Andkilde/Archive Phjotos, (bl) Victor Malafronte/Archive Photos, (bc) Horst Tappe/Archive Photos, (br) Corbis/Kipa; p.21, The Corel Corporation; p. 24, PhotoDisc, Inc.; p. 40, PhotoDisc, Inc.; pp. 41, 93, © Bill Preston; p. 42, George Hunter/Tony Stone Images; p. 48, PhotoDisc, Inc.; p. 50, Image provided by MetaTools; p. 51, Corbis/Phil Schermeister; p. 53, Image provided by MetaTools; p. 62, Printed by permission of the Norman Rockwell Family Trust. © 1949 The Norman Rockwell Family Trust. Photograph courtesy of The Norman Rockwell Museum at Stockbridge; p. 65, Image provided by MetaTools; p. 66, (tl) Charle Gupton/Stock Boston, (tr) Michael Phillip Manheim/The Stock Market, (b) Jon Feingersh/Stock Boston; p. 68, PhotoDisc, Inc.; p. 86, (t) Susan Malis/Marilyn Gartman Agency, (b) Edith G. Haun/Stock Boston; p. 87, Rob Crandall/Stock Boston; p. 88, (tl) Corbis/Bettman, (tm) UPI/Corbis/Bettman, (tr) Corbis/Bettman, (bl) Corbis/Bettman, (bc, br) Corbis Bettman; p. 92, PhotoDisc, Inc.; p. 97, Image provided by MetaTools; p. 98, Courtesy NASA; p. 100, PhotoDisc, Inc.; p. 104, Image provided by MetaTools; p. 113, The Corel Corporation; p. 115, (t) General Motors Media Archives, (b) USDA/PhotoResearchers, Inc.; p. 117, PhotoDisc, Inc.

Cover photos: Earl Ripling/The Stock Rep (cell phone), Jim Barber/The Stock Rep (keyboard), © 1999 Jim Westphalen (type).

Greetings

5.

6.

🎧 The Alphabet

A B C D E F G H I J K L M N O P Q R S T U V W X Y Z

a b c d e f g h i j k l m n o p q r s t u v w x y z

🎧 Things to Know

A: What's this?

B: It's a book.

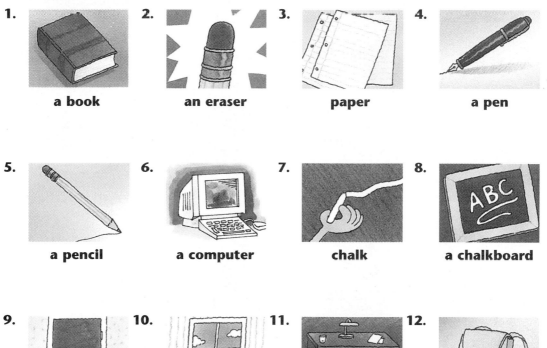

1. **a book**

2. **an eraser**

3. **paper**

4. **a pen**

5. **a pencil**

6. **a computer**

7. **chalk**

8. **a chalkboard**

9. **a door**

10. **a window**

11. **a desk**

12. **a backpack**

13. **a briefcase**

14. **a bus**

15. **a car**

16. **a plane**

Things to Do

1. Stand up. **2.** Sit down. **3.** Raise your hand.

4. Look at picture 1. **5.** Listen. **6.** Repeat. *This is a book.*

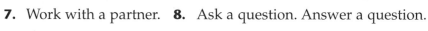

7. Work with a partner. **8.** Ask a question. Answer a question.

Things to Say

1.

2.

3.

GETTING STARTED

Warm Up

1 Work with a partner. Look at the pictures. Ask and answer questions. Use the words in the box.

Example:

A: Look at Number 6. What does he do?

B: He's a taxi driver.

1. a student	**6.** a taxi driver
2. an actress	**7.** a dentist
3. a doctor	**8.** a teacher
4. a secretary	**9.** an actor
5. a nurse	**10.** a pilot

What's your name?

> Good afternoon, ladies and gentlemen, and welcome to the show. I'm Bill Wilson. Let's meet Player One. Player One, please stand up.

2 Listen and read.

A.

BILL: Welcome to *Spell It Right!* I'm your host, Bill Wilson. What's your name, Player One?

CLARE: My name is Clare Taylor.

BILL: Nice to meet you, Clare.

CLARE: Nice to meet you, too, Bill.

BILL: Where are you from, Clare?

CLARE: I'm from Haywood, Wisconsin.

BILL: And what do you do in Haywood?

CLARE: I'm a bus driver.

BILL: Well, welcome to the show.

CLARE: Thanks.

B.

BILL: Are you ready for Word One?

CLARE: Yes, I am.

BILL: OK. Word One is *window*. Please spell *window*.

CLARE: W-I-N-D-O-W.

BILL: That's right! Very good! Word Two is *briefcase*. Please spell *briefcase*.

CLARE: B-R-E-I-F-C-A-S-E.

BILL: Ohhhh. I'm sorry. That's wrong. Player Two, are you ready? ...

3 Circle the correct answer.

a.	Player One is	Clare Taylor	Bill Wilson	Clare Haywood
b.	Haywood is	in Wisconsin	in Mexico	in England
c.	Clare Taylor is	an actress	a taxi driver	a bus driver
d.	The name of the show is	*Say It Right!*	*Spell It Right!*	*That's Right!*
e.	Bill Wilson is	Player One	a bus driver	a TV host

4 Work with a partner. Read and complete the conversations.

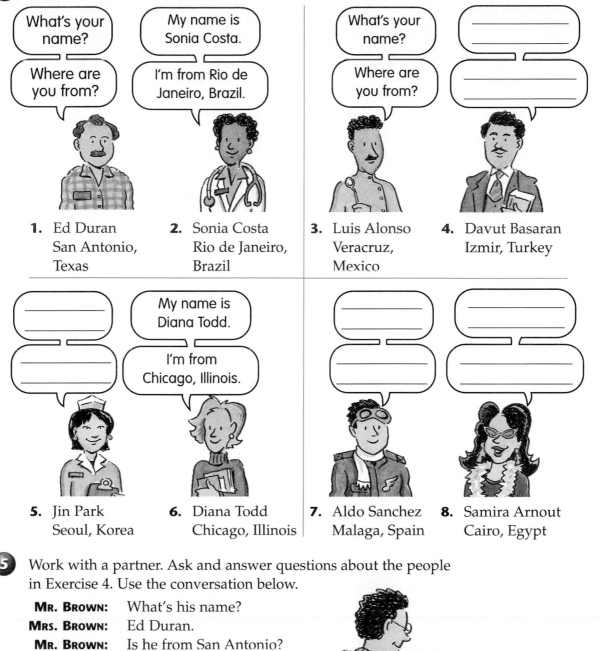

What's your name?

Where are you from?

My name is Sonia Costa.

I'm from Rio de Janeiro, Brazil.

What's your name?

Where are you from?

_____

_____

1. Ed Duran
   San Antonio, Texas

2. Sonia Costa
   Rio de Janeiro, Brazil

3. Luis Alonso
   Veracruz, Mexico

4. Davut Basaran
   Izmir, Turkey

_____

_____

My name is Diana Todd.

I'm from Chicago, Illinois.

_____

_____

_____

_____

5. Jin Park
   Seoul, Korea

6. Diana Todd
   Chicago, Illinois

7. Aldo Sanchez
   Malaga, Spain

8. Samira Arnout
   Cairo, Egypt

5 Work with a partner. Ask and answer questions about the people in Exercise 4. Use the conversation below.

MR. BROWN:	What's his name?
MRS. BROWN:	Ed Duran.
MR. BROWN:	Is he from San Antonio?
MRS. BROWN:	Yes, he is.
MR. BROWN:	What's her name?
MRS. BROWN:	Sonia Costa.
MR. BROWN:	Is she from Costa Rica?
MRS. BROWN:	No, she's not. She's from Brazil.

Building Vocabulary
Occupations

 6 Listen and read.

an actor	an athlete	a taxi driver	a singer
an actress	a doctor	a pilot	a writer

7 Work with a partner. Look at the pictures. Ask and answer questions about the people. Use *he* or *she*.

Example:

A: What does she do?

B: She's an actress.

a.   b.   c.   d.

e.   f.   g.   h.

Numbers

 8 Listen to the numbers. Practice them with a partner.

1 one	5 five	9 nine	13 thirteen	17 seventeen
2 two	6 six	10 ten	14 fourteen	18 eighteen
3 three	7 seven	11 eleven	15 fifteen	19 nineteen
4 four	8 eight	12 twelve	16 sixteen	20 twenty

9 Work with a partner. Add the numbers.

Example:

$6 + 2 = 8$

A: What's six and two?

B: Six and two is eight.

a. $4 + 8 = ?$ c. $7 + 1 = ?$ e. $3 + 12 = ?$ g. $9 + 7 = ?$ i. $2 + 11 = ?$

b. $12 + 5 = ?$ d. $8 + 6 = ?$ f. $10 + 9 = ?$ h. $1 + 6 = ?$ j. $13 + 5 = ?$

Talk About It

10 Work with a partner. Make statements about the people on page 3. Complete the chart.

Example:

Number 1 is Ed Duran. He's from San Antonio, Texas. He's a taxi driver.

Name	From	Occupation
1. Ed Duran	*San Antonio, Texas*	a taxi driver
2.	Rio de Janeiro, Brazil	
3. Luis Alonso		a dentist
4.	Izmir, Turkey	
5. Jin Park	Seoul, Korea	
6.	Chicago, Illinois	a student
7. Aldo Sanchez		
8.		an actress

GRAMMAR

The Simple Present Tense: Statements with *Be*

We use the simple present tense of *be* to talk about people and places.

Affirmative	Negative	
I **am** from Mexico City.	I **am** (I'**m**) **not** from Brazil.	
You **are** from Egypt.	You **are** (You'**re**) **not** from Japan.	You **aren't** from Brazil.
Barcelona **is** in Spain.	It **is** (It'**s**) **not** in Peru.	It **isn't** in Brazil.
He **is** a doctor.	He **is** (He'**s**) **not** a nurse.	He **isn't** a nurse.
They **are** students.	They **are** (They'**re**) **not** teachers.	They **aren't** teachers.

note Contractions:
I am = I'm
you are = you're
it is = it's
he is = he's
they are = they're

note Negative contractions:
is not = isn't
are not = aren't

1 Complete the sentences with the simple present tense of *be*.

My name **(1.)** ___is___ Clare Taylor. I **(2.)** _____ from Haywood. Haywood **(3.)** _____ in Wisconsin. I **(4.)** _____ not a secretary. I **(5.)** _____ a taxi driver.

2 Write five sentences about yourself. Read your sentences to a partner.

Unit 1

5

Yes/No Questions with *Be*

Yes/No Questions	Short Answers	
	Affirmative	*Negative*
Are you from Rio de Janeiro?	Yes, I **am**.	No, I**'m not**.
Is she a taxi driver?	Yes, she **is**.	No, she **isn't**./No, she**'s not**.
Are the Browns from Madrid?	Yes, they **are**.	No, they **aren't**./No, they**'re not**.
Are you doctors?	Yes, we **are**.	No, we **aren't**./No, we**'re not**.

note **Contractions:** she is = she's
  we are = we're

3 Work with a partner. Practice the conversations.

DIANA: Are you from Spain?
SAMIRA: No, I'm not. I'm from Egypt.
DIANA: Are you an actress?
SAMIRA: Yes, I am.

LUIS: Is Jin from Korea?
DAVUT: Yes, she is.
LUIS: Is she a dentist?
DAVUT: No, she isn't. She's a nurse.

JIN: Are Ed and Diana from the
United States?
ALDO: Yes, they are.
JIN: Are they from Dallas?
ALDO: No, they're not.

4 Complete the conversation with the correct form of *be*.

ED: (1.) _____*Are*_____ you from Turkey?
DAVUT: Yes, I (2.)_____. (3.)_____ you
from California?
ED: Me? No, I (4. *neg.*) _____.
I (5.) _____ from San Antonio.
DAVUT: (6.) _____ San Antonio in New Mexico?
ED: No, it (7. *neg.*) _____. It (8.) _____ in Texas.
DAVUT: (9.) _____ El Paso in Texas?
ED: Yes, it (10.) _____. San Antonio and El Paso
(11.) _____ in Texas. They (12. *neg.*) _____
in New Mexico.

5 Work with a partner. Ask and answer questions about the people.

Example:

A: Is Michele Kwan an actress?

B: No, she's not. She's an athlete.

a. Michele Kwan
United States
athlete (ice skater)

b. Ricky Martin
Puerto Rico
singer

c. Se Ri Pak
Korea
athlete (golfer)

d. Antonio Banderas
Spain
actor

e. Isabelle Allende
Chile
writer

f. Gong Li
China
actress

Information Questions with *Be*

Information Questions	Possible Answers
What is your name?	My name **is** Clara.
What's his name?	His name **is** Ed.
Where are you from?	I**'m** from New York.
Where's she from?	She**'s** from Canada.
Where are they from?	They**'re** from the United States.

note **Contractions:**
what is = what's
where is = where's

6 Read the answers. Write the questions. Use contractions.

Luis:	(1.) <u>What's your name</u>?		**Jin:**	(3.) _____?
Sonia:	My name is Sonia.		**Aldo:**	His name is Ed.
Luis:	(2.) _____?		**Jin:**	(4.) _____?
Sonia:	I'm from Egypt.		**Aldo:**	Her name is Diana.
			Jin:	(5.) _____?
			Aldo:	They're from the United States.

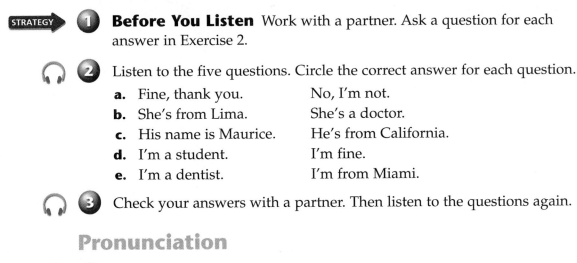

7 **Express Yourself** Work with a partner. Ask questions. Tell the class about your partner.

Example:

His name is Carlos. He's from Lima. Lima is in Peru. He's not a bus driver. He's a student.

LISTENING and SPEAKING

Listen: What's the Answer?

STRATEGY **1** **Before You Listen** Work with a partner. Ask a question for each answer in Exercise 2.

2 Listen to the five questions. Circle the correct answer for each question.

a.	Fine, thank you.	No, I'm not.
b.	She's from Lima.	She's a doctor.
c.	His name is Maurice.	He's from California.
d.	I'm a student.	I'm fine.
e.	I'm a dentist.	I'm from Miami.

3 Check your answers with a partner. Then listen to the questions again.

Pronunciation

4 Listen and read.

> **Intonation with Yes/No Questions**
>
> Yes/No questions usually have rising intonation.
>
> Are you a student? Is he from Turkey?

5 Listen and repeat the questions. Use rising intonation.

a.	Are you a teacher?	**d.**	Is Jin a doctor?
b.	Is she an actress?	**e.**	Are you from Korea?
c.	Are they from Brazil?	**f.**	Are we students?

Speak Out

6 Complete the conversation between Mario and Jim. Cross out Jim's incorrect answers.

MARIO	JIM
a. Good morning.	Good morning. ~~I'm fine, thank you.~~
b. I'm Mario Ortiz.	I'm from Seattle. My name is Jim Hanson.
c. Nice to meet you, Jim.	What do you do, Mario? Nice to meet you, too. Where are you from?
d. I'm from Los Angeles.	I'm from Chicago. What do you do? I'm sorry. I'm not from Los Angeles.
e. I'm an English teacher.	I'm a taxi driver, too. I'm a writer.

7 Work with a partner. Practice the conversation.

STRATEGY **Asking Someone to Spell a Word** To ask someone to spell a word, you say:

> **JIM:** How do you spell *Ortiz*?
>
> **MARIO:** O-R-T-I-Z.

8 Practice the conversation. Use information about yourselves. Ask your partner to spell his or her last name.

READING and WRITING

Read About It

STRATEGY

1 **Before You Read** What is a pen pal? Do you have a pen pal?

2 Masao and Flora are pen pals. Read Masao's postcard to Flora.

Dear Flora,

How are you? My name is Masao Omachi. I'm from Tokyo, Japan. I'm a student. What do you do? Please be my pen pal and write to me. Tell me about yourself.

Sincerely,

Masao

Flora Fernandez
Nicanor Arteaga 707
Lima 41, Peru
South America

3 Answer the questions.

    a. Where is Masao from?   **c.** What does he do?

    b. Is Masao a secretary?   **d.** Where is Flora from?

Write About It

 4 **Before You Write** Finish Flora's postcard to Masao. Use the words in the box.

fine	write
be	Thank you
bus driver	are

> Dear Masao,
>
> _____ for your postcard!
> I'm _____, thanks. How
> _____ you? I'm a
> _____ in Lima, Peru. I'm
> happy to _____ your pen
> pal. Please _____ again!
>   Best wishes,
>
>   Flora
>
>   Masao Omachi
>   Gyokuroen Building
>   1-13-19 Sekiguchi
>   Bunkyo-ku, Tokyo 112
>   Tokyo, Japan

5 **Write** Write a postcard to a pen pal about yourself.

> Dear _____ ,
>
> _____
> _____
> _____
> _____
> _____
> _____
>   Best wishes,
>
>   _____

 6 **Check Your Writing** Work with a partner. Read your partner's postcard. Correct your sentences. Write the final copy.

- Are the simple present tense verbs correct?
- Is the spelling correct?

GETTING STARTED

Warm Up

1 Work with a partner. Look at the pictures. Ask, *What do they do?*
Where do they work? Write the numbers.

a. __3__ He's a doctor.
She's a nurse.
They work at a hospital.

b. ____ They're musicians.
The boy plays the drums.
The girl plays the guitar.

c. ____ They're clerks.
They don't work in an office.
They work in a hotel.

d. ____ The man is an actor.
The woman is an actress.
They work in a theater.

e. ____ He's a piano teacher.
He doesn't work at a school.
He works in a theater, too.

f. ____ They're secretaries.
They work in an office.

Is this the flight to Chicago?

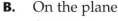 **2** Listen and read.

A. At the airport in London

KENJI: Is this the flight to Chicago?

CLERK: Yes, it is. Do you have your ticket?

KENJI: Yes, I do. Here it is.

CLERK: Thank you. Is your name Kenji Miula?

KENJI: Well, my first name is Kenji, but my last name is Miura.

CLERK: Spell your last name, please.

KENJI: M-I-U-R-A.

CLERK: Thank you. Do you live in London?

KENJI: Yes, I do. I study English here.

CLERK: OK, Mr. Miura. Do you have a suitcase?

KENJI: Yes, I do. I have a guitar and a backpack, too. Here they are.

CLERK: Thank you. Have a nice flight.

KENJI: Thanks.

B. On the plane

ATTENDANT: Ladies and gentlemen, may I have your forms, please?

KENJI: Excuse me. What does *occupation* mean?

ATTENDANT: What do you do, sir?

KENJI: I'm a student.

ATTENDANT: Then your occupation is "student."

KENJI: And what about nationality?

ATTENDANT: Where are you from?

KENJI: Japan.

ATTENDANT: Then write "Japanese."

KENJI: Thank you.

ATTENDANT: You're welcome.

C. At the airport in Chicago

CLERK: Passport, please.

KENJI: Here you are.

CLERK: What's your name?

KENJI: Kenji Miura. M-I-U-R-A.

CLERK: What's your occupation, Mr. Miura?

KENJI: I'm a student.

CLERK: Are you in the United States on business?

KENJI: No, I'm not. I'm on vacation.

CLERK: What's your address in Chicago?

KENJI: 15 School Street.

CLERK: Is that a hotel?

KENJI: No, it's not. My friend Dr. Yatabe lives there.

CLERK: Thank you, Mr. Miura. Welcome to Chicago. Have a nice vacation.

> Welcome to Chicago/
> O'Hare International Airport
>
> United States
> Customs

Unit 2

3 Read the sentences. Circle **T** for True or **F** for False.
Correct the false sentences.

a.	Kenji is from London.	T	Ⓕ	*Kenji is from Japan.*
b.	The flight is from London.	T	F	_____
c.	The flight is to Chicago.	T	F	_____
d.	Kenji lives in London.	T	F	_____
e.	Kenji has a briefcase.	T	F	_____
f.	Kenji is a teacher.	T	F	_____
g.	Kenji is in Chicago on business.	T	F	_____
h.	Dr. Yatabe lives in Chicago.	T	F	

4 Work with a partner. Ask and answer
questions about Kenji. Use the words in
the box.

a ticket	a suitcase
a passport	a backpack
a postcard	an address in Chicago
a briefcase	a guitar

Example:

A: Does Kenji have a ticket?

B: Yes, he does. Does he have
a briefcase?

A: No, he doesn't.

Building Vocabulary

Places and People

  5 Listen and read.

Places			**People**		
airport	city	office	man	musician	friend
school	theater	hotel	boy	flight attendant	woman
hospital	Street		clerk	girl	pilot

6 Complete the sentences. Use words from Exercise 5.

a. She's a ____pilot____. She works on a plane.

b. They're doctors. They work at a _____.

c. He's a teacher. He works at a _____.

d. They're actors. They work in a _____.

e. She's a secretary. She works in an _____.

f. He's a _____. He plays a guitar.

g. She's a _____. She works in a hotel.

h. Kenji has a _____ in Chicago.
His name is Dr. Yatabe.

i. Dr. Yatabe lives in Chicago. His address is
15 School _____.

j. Chicago is a big _____. It's
in the United States.

In, On, At

 7 Listen and read.

The book is **in** the desk.   The book is **on** the desk.   The teacher is **at** the chalkboard.

8 Look at the picture. Complete the sentences with *in, on,* or *at.*

a. The teacher is __at__ the window.
b. The briefcase is _____ the desk.
c. The papers are _____ the briefcase.
d. The boy is _____ the chalkboard.
e. The girl is _____ the door.
f. The guitar is _____ the chair.
g. The books are _____ the backpack.
h. The number is _____ the door.

Talk About It

9 Ask your classmates about the things in the boxes. Find a person who has each of the things. Write the classmate's name in the box. When you have four names in a row, say, *Bingo.* The first person to say *Bingo* wins.

Example:

A: Do you have a guitar?
B: Yes, I do.

B	I	N	G	O
a guitar	a suitcase	a computer	an eraser
a briefcase	a backpack	a piano	a pencil
a passport	an English book	a postcard	a ticket
a pen pal	a pen	a TV	a drum

GRAMMAR

A, An

We use *a* or *an* with singular nouns. We don't use *a* or *an* with plural nouns.

Singular Nouns	Plural Nouns
She's **a teacher**.	We **are teachers**.
He's **an actor**.	They **are actors**.

We use *a* before a consonant sound. Use *an* before a vowel sound.

Aldo Sanchez is **a p**ilot.	Samira Amout is **an a**ctress.
Sonia Costa works in **a h**ospital.	Diana Todd works in **an o**ffice.

1 Work with a partner. Say each word in the box. Then make sentences. Use *a* or *an*.

Example:

A: Backpack.

B: He has a backpack. Actress.

A: She's an actress. Ticket.

backpack	actress
ticket	actor
theater	friend
airport	answer
athlete	hospital
musician	question

Singular and Plural Nouns

Most plural nouns end in *–s*, *–es*, or *–ies*.

a ticket   ticket**s**   an actress   actress**es**   a secretary   secretar**ies**

Some plural nouns are irregular.

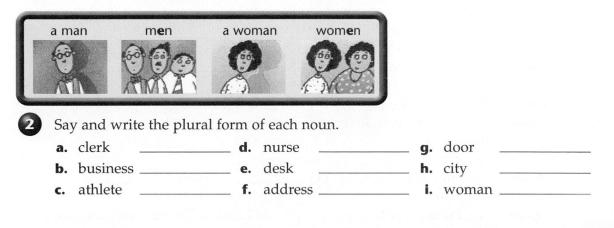

a man   m**e**n   a woman   wom**e**n

2 Say and write the plural form of each noun.

a. clerk _____   d. nurse _____   g. door _____

b. business _____   e. desk _____   h. city _____

c. athlete _____   f. address _____   i. woman _____

The Simple Present Tense

We use the simple present tense to talk about everyday activities.

Singular	Plural
I **work** in a hotel.	We **work** in a hospital.
She **works** in an office.	Bob and Evan **live** in Brazil.
He **doesn't play** the drums.	They **don't speak** English.

note **Contractions:** does not = doesn't   do not = don't

We use *do* or *does* to ask yes/no questions and to give short answers.

Yes/No Questions	Short Answers
Does she **live** in Brazil?	Yes, she **does**./No, she **doesn't**.
Does it **work**?	Yes, it **does**./No, it **doesn't**.
Do you **speak** Spanish?	Yes, we **do**./No, we **don't**.
Do they **have** backpacks?	Yes, they **do**./No, they **don't**.

note *You* can be singular or plural.

3 Kenji meets his friend, Dr. Hiroshi Yatabe. Complete the conversation with the correct form of the verbs in the box.

> live   play   speak   work

KENJI: Hi, Hiroshi. How are you?

HIROSHI: I'm fine, thanks. Kenji, this is Anna. She **(1.)** ___works___ at Mercy Hospital in Chicago. She's a secretary.

KENJI: Nice to meet you, Anna. Do you **(2.)** _____ Japanese?

ANNA: Not very well. I'm from New York. I **(3.)** _____ English.

HIROSHI: Kenji, this is my friend, Junko and his friend, Reiko. They **(4.)** _____ in Chicago, too. Junko is a musician.

KENJI: Hi, Junko. Nice to meet you. **(5.)** _____ you _____ in a theater?

JUNKO: Yes, I do. Reiko **(6.)** _____ in a theater, too. She's an actress.

KENJI: Nice to meet you, Reiko. I'm a musician, too. I **(7.)** _____ the guitar.

HIROSHI: Junko **(8.)** _____ the piano.

REIKO: Nice to meet you, Kenji. **(9.)** _____ you _____ in Japan?

KENJI: No, I don't. I **(10.)** _____ in London. I'm here on vacation.

4 Work with a partner. Look at the picture. Ask and answer the questions.

Example:

A: Does Kenji have a guitar?

B: Yes, he does. Does Kenji have a drum?

A: No, he doesn't.

a. Does Kenji have his backpack?
b. Does Kenji work at an airport?
c. Do the pilots have suitcases?
d. Do the pilots have guitars?
e. Does Kenji play the guitar?
f. Does Kenji have a suitcase?
g. Do the pilots work at an airport?

Do you have my backpack?

The Simple Present Tense: Information Questions

In most information questions, we use *do* or *does* after the question word.

Questions	Answers
Where do you live?	I live in Caracas.
Where does he work?	He works in a hospital.
What do they do?	They're doctors.

5 Work with a partner. Look at Exercise 3. Ask and answer information questions.

Example:

A: Where does Kenji live?

B: He lives in London.

a. What/Kenji do?
b. What/Kenji study?
c. Where/Hiroshi and Anna live?
d. What/Reiko do?
e. Where/Reiko work?
f. What/Hiroshi do?
g. What/Anna do?
h. Where/Anna work?

 6 **Express Yourself** Work with a partner. Ask and answer questions. Use the words in the box.

speak	work	play	live	have

Example:

A: Do you work in a hospital?

B: No, I don't.

LISTENING and SPEAKING

Listen: Where Do They Work?

STRATEGY **1** **Before You Listen** Look at the pictures in Exercise 2. Name the places.

2 Listen to the sentences. Write the correct name on the line.

Tom	Allen	Bill
Maria	Ann	Mario

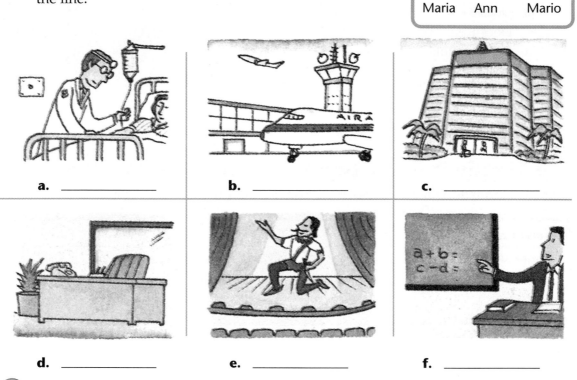

a. _____

b. _____

c. _____

d. _____

e. _____

f. _____

3 Check your answers in Exercise 2 with a partner. Then listen to the sentences again.

Pronunciation

4 Listen and read.

> **Plural Nouns**
>
> We pronounce plural endings in three ways.
>
> | /s/ | | /z/ | | /ɪz/ | |
> |-----|------|------|-------|-------|----------|
> | ticket | ticke**ts** | friend | frien**ds** | actress | actres**ses** |

5 Listen and repeat each pair of words.

  a. clerk/clerks   d. class/classes
  b. secretary/secretaries e. flight/flights
  c. address/addresses   f. drum/drums

Speak Out

6 Complete the conversation. Match the question in Column A with the correct answer in Column B.

Column A

_____ What's your name?

_____ Where do you live?

_____ What's your address?

_____ What's your occupation?

_____ What do you study?

_____ Where do you study?

Column B

a. At New York University.

b. I'm a student.

c. Allen Barnett.

d. 12 Spring Street.

e. I live in New York City.

f. I study Spanish.

7 Work with a partner. Write the conversation in Exercise 6. Then practice the conversation.

STRATEGY ▶ **Asking Someone to Repeat Information** To ask someone to repeat information, you can say:

> **A:** Excuse me, what's your last name again, please?
>
> **B:** Barnett.

8 Practice the conversation again. Use your own information. Ask your partner to repeat his or her name.

READING and WRITING

Read About It

STRATEGY ▶ **1** **Before You Read** Look at Exercise 3 on page 16. Where do Hiroshi and Anna live? What does Anna do? Where does she work?

The Yatabes

Hiroshi and Anna Yatabe live in Chicago. Their address is 15 School Street. They live on the second floor.

Hiroshi is from Japan. He speaks English and Japanese. He's a doctor. He works at Mercy Hospital.

Anna works at Mercy Hospital, too, but she's not a doctor. She's a secretary. Her office is on the first floor. She fills in forms for the doctors and nurses. Anna is from New York. She speaks English. She understands some Japanese, but she doesn't speak it very well.

Hiroshi and Anna are musicians, too. Hiroshi plays the guitar and Anna plays the piano. They play music or listen to music on the radio every night after work.

second floor

first floor

2 Complete the passport form for Hiroshi.

Name: _____
     First   Last

Address: _____
        Street   City

Nationality: _____

Occupation: _____

Works at: _____

Write About It

STRATEGY **3** **Before You Write** Complete this form. Use information about yourself.

Name: _____
     First   Last

Address: _____
        Street   City

Nationality: _____

Occupation: _____

Languages: _____

Work/Study at: _____

4 **Write** Use the form to write five sentences about yourself.

 5 **Check Your Writing** Work with a partner. Read each other's sentences. Correct your sentences. Write the final copy.

- Are *a* and *an* correct?
- Are the simple present tense verbs correct?
- Is the spelling correct?

Carol Cook   Carlos Garcia   Rosa Hanson   John Fratelli

Miguel Garcia   Gina Fratelli

Mimi Garcia   Anna Garcia   Antonio Garcia

Carlos is Miguel's father.
Carol is Miguel's mother.
Gina is Miguel's wife.

Miguel is Gina's husband.
Anna and Mimi are Miguel and Gina's daughters.
Antonio is Miguel and Gina's son.
Mimi is Anna's sister.

Antonio is Anna's brother.
Rosa is Anna's grandmother.
John is Anna's grandfather.
Anna and Mimi are Carol and Carlos's granddaughters.
Antonio is Carol and Carlos's grandson.

GETTING STARTED

Warm Up

1 Fill in the form for yourself.

1. Name: _____

2. Mother's name: _____

3. Father's name: _____

4. Address: _____
        number   street   city

5. Grandmothers' names: _____

6. Grandfathers' names: _____

7. *(Check the true sentences. Write the numbers.)*

☐ I don't have a brother.   ☐ I don't have a sister.

☐ I have one brother   ☐ I have one sister.

☐ I have ____ brothers.   ☐ I have ____ sisters.

Can you read it?

 2 Listen and read.

A. **PROFESSOR:** Good morning. My name is Darla Williams. I am a botanist and I study plants. This morning my talk is about rhubarb. This is *Rheum rhabarbarum* or rhubarb. Rhubarb is a very interesting plant.

KEN: Excuse me, Professor. I can't spell *rhubarb*. Please write it on the board.

PROFESSOR: Of course. It's R-H-U-B-A-R-B. Can you read it?

KEN: Yes, I can. Thank you.

B. **PROFESSOR:** Here's something interesting. Rhubarb is poisonous.

MARIA: Excuse me, Professor. Rhubarb isn't poisonous. My grandmother makes rhubarb pies. We eat the pies, and we aren't dead!

PROFESSOR: Rhubarb is poisonous, but your grandmother's pies aren't poisonous. I can explain. Does your grandmother cook the stalks or the leaves?

MARIA: She cooks the stalks.

PROFESSOR: That's very important. You can cook and eat rhubarb stalks, but you can't eat the leaves.

MARIA: So, rhubarb leaves are poisonous, but my grandmother's rhubarb pies aren't! That's very interesting.

3 Answer the questions.

a. What is the professor's name?
b. What does a botanist study?
c. Can the professor spell *rhubarb*?
d. What does Maria's grandmother make?
e. Can you eat the leaves of rhubarb?
f. Is rhubarb poisonous? Explain.

pie

4 Read the sentences. Circle **T** for True or **F** for False. Correct the false sentences.

Example:

The professor's name is Maria. T (F) *The professor's name is Darla Williams.*

a. Rhubarb is a plant. T F _____
b. The professor is a botanist. T F _____
c. Ken can spell *rhubarb*. T F _____
d. Rhubarb stalks are poisonous. T F _____
e. Rhubarb pies are poisonous. T F _____
f. You can eat rhubarb stalks. T F _____

Unit 3

22

Building Vocabulary

Activities

 5 Look at the pictures. Listen and read.

a. sing   **b.** drive a bus   **c.** ride a bike   **d.** write

e. read   **f.** run   **g.** use a computer   **h.** dance

i. swim   **j.** walk   **k.** cook   **l.** speak Spanish

6 Work with a partner. Ask and answer questions about the people in Exercise 5.

Example:

A: Look at picture **f**. What can she do?

B: She can run. Look at picture **g**. What can they do?

Numbers

7 Listen to the numbers. Practice them with a partner.

21 twenty one	76 seventy-six
32 thirty-two	87 eighty-seven
43 forty-three	98 ninety-eight
54 fifty-four	100 one hundred
65 sixty-five	1,000 one thousand

Talk About It

8 Work with a partner. Ask and answer questions about your families. Use the form on page 21.

Example:

A: What's your mother's name?

B: My mother's name is Susan. What's your mother's name?

GRAMMAR

Can/Can't

We use *can* to talk about ability.

Questions	Answers	
	Affirmative	*Negative*
Can you **speak** Japanese?	Yes, I **can**.	**No**, I **can't**.
Can we **play** the piano?	Yes, we **can**.	**No**, we **can't**.
What can he **do**?	He **can** play football.	He **can't** swim.
What can they **do**?	They **can** dance.	They **can't** sing.

note **Contractions:** can not = can't

1 What can you do? Check (✓) the line. Work with a partner. What can your partner do? Check (✓) the line.

Example:

A: Can you swim?

B: Yes, I can.

	I can	My partner can
a. swim	_____	_____
b. ride a bike	_____	_____
c. sing in English	_____	_____
d. drive a car	_____	_____
e. make a pie	_____	_____
f. read Japanese	_____	_____
g. speak French	_____	_____
h. cook	_____	_____
i. play the guitar	_____	_____
j. use a computer	_____	_____

2 Work in groups of four. Talk about your partner from Exercise 1.
Example:
Ana can swim. She can't cook.

And, But, Or

And	I can swim.
	I can drive, too.
	I can swim **and** drive.
But	He can dance.
	He can't sing.
	He can dance, **but** he can't sing.
Or	John and Sue can't swim.
	John and Sue can't ride bikes.
	John and Sue can't swim **or** ride bikes.

3 Complete the conversation with *and, but,* or *or.* Then work with a
partner. Practice the conversation.

EVAN: Are you a musician?
LUIS: No, I'm not. I can't play the guitar
       (1.) _or_ read music.
EVAN: Can you sing **(2.)** _____ dance?
LUIS: No, I can't, **(3.)** _____ my brother can sing
       (4.) _____ dance.
EVAN: That's interesting. Can you drive a bus?
LUIS: No, I can't drive a bus **(5.)** _____ a car,
       (6.) _____ I can ride a bike.
EVAN: Can you cook?
LUIS: No, I can't cook, **(7.)** _____ I can eat!
EVAN: Can you use a computer?
LUIS: No, I can't, **(8.)** _____ my brother can. He can read **(9.)** _____
       write music, too.
EVAN: Can I talk to your brother?
LUIS: Yes!
EVAN: Can you write your brother's name and address on this paper?
LUIS: I can write his name, **(10.)** _____ I don't know his address. He
       lives in Australia!
EVAN: Oh!

4 Work in groups of four. Talk about your partner from Exercise 1.
Make sentences with *and, but,* or *or.*

Example: Carlos can cook, but he can't make a pie.

This/That

Use *this* to talk about something that is close to you. Use *that* to talk about something that is not close to you.

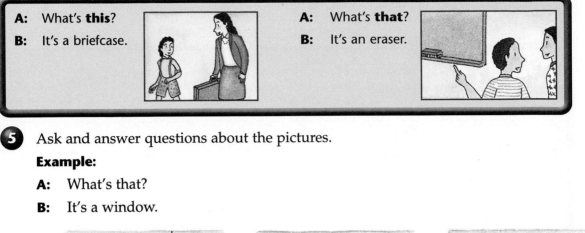

A: What's **this**?

B: It's a briefcase.

A: What's **that**?

B: It's an eraser.

5 Ask and answer questions about the pictures.

Example:

A: What's that?

B: It's a window.

a.

b.

c.

d.

e.

f.

Possessive Nouns

David has a briefcase.	Here is **David's** briefcase.
Carl and Alison have a car.	This is Carl and **Alison's** car.
Charles has two brothers.	**Charles's** brothers are Tom and Joe.
I have two sisters.	My **sisters'** names are Ellen and Sonia.

 note

Singular	Plural
man's	men's
woman's	women's
secretary's	secretaries'
wife's	wives'
actress's	actresses'

6 Read about Charles's family. Fill in the names on his family tree.

    a. Melanie is Charles's mother.   **e.** Melanie is Linda's daughter.
    b. Paul is Melanie's husband.   **f.** Michael and John are Charles's grandfathers.
    c. John is Paul's father.   **g.** Tracy is Charles's sister.
    d. Marian is John's wife.   **h.** Tracy's brothers' names are Charles and David.

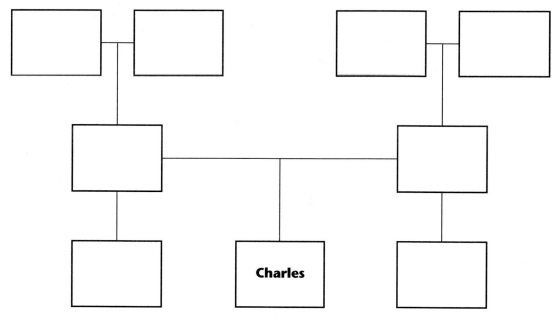

 7 **Express Yourself** Complete the chart about your family. (✓ = can, ✗ = can't)

	father	mother	sister	brother	grandmother	grandfather
make a pie						
sing						
ride a bike						
use a computer						
cook						
dance						
drive						
swim						
play the piano						

8 Work in small groups. Talk about your family. Use *and, but,* and *or.*

Example:

    A: My mother can cook.

    B: My father can dance, *but* he can't sing.

    C: My brother can't sing *or* dance.

Listen: Can He Run?

STRATEGY ➤ **1** **Before You Listen** Look at the pictures. What can you do? What can't you do?

2 Listen to each sentence. Circle **T** for True or **F** for False for each picture.

1. a. T   F   **2. a. T   F**   **3. a. T   F**   **4. a. T   F**

b. T   F   **b. T   F**   **b. T   F**   **b. T   F**

3 Listen again and check your answers.

Pronunciation

4 Listen and read.

Possessive Nouns

We pronounce possessive nouns in three ways.

/s/	/z/	/ɪz/
attendan**t's**	mothe**r's**	actres**s's**
cler**k's**	secretar**y's**	clas**s's**
wi**fe's**	gir**l's**	Charle**s's**

5 Listen. Circle the correct word.

a.	actor	actor's	**d.**	friend	friend's	**g.**	pilot	pilot's
b.	brother	brother's	**e.**	woman	woman's	**h.**	sister	sister's
c.	dentist	dentist's	**f.**	nurse	nurse's	**i.**	address	addresses

Speak Out

6 Number the sentences in the correct order. Make a conversation.

_____ **a.** Her name is Julie.

_____ **b.** No, she can't play the piano, but she can play the guitar.

_1_ **c.** Helen, do you have a sister?

_____ **d.** Can she play the piano?

_____ **e.** Yes, I do.

_____ **f.** What's your sister's name?

STRATEGY **Can and Can't** Listen to *can* and *can't* in this sentence.

 She **can't** play the piano, but she can play the guitar.

 note *Can't* is stressed.
Can is not stressed.

7 Work with a partner. Read the conversation in Exercise 6. Use correct stress on *can't*.

8 Practice the conversation again. Use your own information.

READING and WRITING

Read About It

 STRATEGY **1** **Before You Read** Look at the pictures. Do you eat potatoes, tomatoes, or tobacco? What plant family is the reading about?

A Plant Family

Do you eat tomatoes and potatoes? Tomato and potato plants are in the nightshade family. *Atropa belladonna*, or deadly nightshade, is in that family, too. Deadly nightshade is very poisonous. You can die if you eat a deadly nightshade plant.

Tomato and potato plants are also poisonous. You can eat potatoes and tomatoes, but you can't eat the leaves of these plants.

Tobacco is in the nightshade family, too. Tobacco leaves have nicotine in them. Nicotine is very poisonous. You can eat tobacco leaves if you cook them. You can smoke tobacco leaves, too, but doctors say, "Tobacco is poisonous. Don't smoke!"

potato

tomato

tobacco leaves

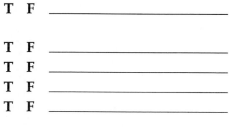

Don't smoke.

2 Read the sentences. Circle **T** for True and **F** for False. Correct the false statements.

    a. Tomatoes, potatoes, and tobacco are in one plant family.   **T** **F** _____

    b. You can eat the leaves of the tomato plant.   **T** **F** _____

    c. You can't eat the leaves of the potato plant.   **T** **F** _____

    d. Tobacco leaves are poisonous.   **T** **F** _____

    e. Nicotine is in tomato leaves.   **T** **F** _____

Write About It

 3 Read the paragraph about Mouneer's family. Then complete Mouneer's family tree.

> My name is Mouneer. I live in Cairo, Egypt. I'm a dentist. My wife's name is Mona. We have a son and a daughter. Our daughter's name is Mouneera. My son's name is Sami. My father and mother live in Alexandria, Egypt. My father's name is Rauf. My mother's name is Fatima. Mona's mother and father live in Alexandria, too. Her mother's name is Aziza. Her father's name is Hassan.

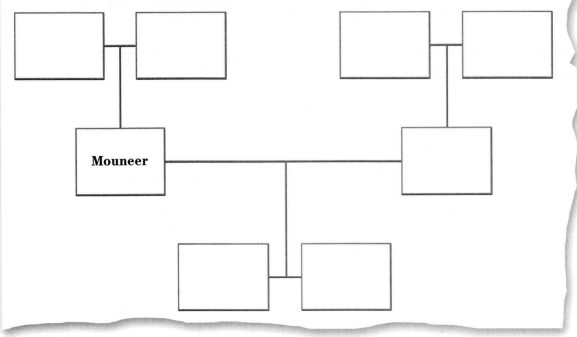

Mouneer

  4 **Before You Write** Make a family tree for your family.

5 **Write** Write a paragraph about your family. Use Mouneer's paragraph and your family tree as models.

☑ **6** **Check Your Writing** Work with a partner. Read each other's paragraphs. Correct your sentences. Write the final copy.

- Are the possessive nouns correct?
- Is the spelling correct?

1 Complete the conversation with the simple present tense of *be*. You can use contractions.

ANDRE: Welcome to the show, *People and Places*. My name **(1.)** _____ Andre Perout, and I **(2.)** _____ your host today. Meet Player One.

ELLA: Hi, Andre. I **(3.)** _____ Ella Dodge.

ANDRE: It **(4.)** _____ nice to meet you, Ella. Where **(5.)** _____ you from?

ELLA: I **(6.)** _____ from the United States, Andre. But my family **(7. neg.)** _____.

ANDRE: Where **(8.)** _____ they from?

ELLA: Oh, they **(9.)** _____ from Peru.

ANDRE: How interesting! And Kim Lui **(10. neg.)** _____ you from the United States?

KIM: Yes, I **(11.)** _____ , Andre.

ANDRE: And your family? Where **(12.)** _____ they from?

KIM: Japan.

2 Complete the conversation with the simple present tense of the verbs.

ANNA: Good morning. **(1. be)** _____ this Music City?

CLERK: Yes.

ANNA: **(2. have)** _____ you _____ pianos?

CLERK: Of course, we **(3. have)** _____ pianos. **(4. play)** _____ you _____ the piano?

ANNA: No, I **(5. do, neg.)** _____, but my sister **(6. do)** _____. She **(7. sing)** _____ and she **(8. write)** _____ music, too.

CLERK: What about you?

ANNA: Oh, I **(9. write, neg.)** _____ music and I **(10. sing, neg.)** _____.

3 Complete the sentences with *and, but,* or *or.*

1. I have a sister _____ two brothers.

2. Sheila can speak Spanish, _____ she can't read Spanish.

3. Carmen lives in Mexico, _____ she doesn't live in Mexico City.

4. Is the secretary a man _____ a woman?

5. Please write your name _____ address.

6. Anton doesn't have a briefcase _____ a backpack.

7. Emil works in a hotel, _____ he's not a clerk.

8. Do you walk to school _____ ride your bike?

4 Complete the sentences with the correct possessive nouns.

Example:

Tom _____Tom's_____ last name is Brown.

1. *secretary* The _____ papers are on her desk.

2. *student* The _____ books are at school.

3. *brothers* My _____ names are James and Richard.

4. *women* Where are the _____ hats?

5. *wife* His _____ sister lives in Brazil.

6. *actress* The _____ address is 12 Bank Street.

7. *man* Excuse me. Do you have the _____ suitcase?

8. *David* _____ backpack is on his chair.

9. *Thomas* _____ mother and father are on vacation.

10. *musicians* The _____ drums are at the theater.

5 Complete the sentences with *in, at,* or *on.*

1. Kim's papers are _____ her backpack.

2. Yoko's hat is _____ her head.

3. Ruth's parents are _____ vacation.

4. The student is _____ the chalkboard.

5. Sally and her brother are _____ a taxi.

6. Michelle is _____ work today.

7. The theater is _____ State Street.

8. The doctor's name is _____ the door.

Vocabulary Review

Complete the sentences with words from the box.

driver	friend
nurse	family
address	backpack
airport	ticket
city	hotel

1. My _____ and her husband live in Canada.

2. Angela works at the hospital. She's a _____.

3. Does your brother's _____ live in the United States?

4. Please have your _____ ready for the flight attendant.

5. I'm sorry. The bus _____ doesn't speak English.

6. Cuzco is an old _____ in Peru.

7. Annabelle is a pilot. She works at the _____.

8. Eli is a night clerk at the _____.

9. What is your _____?

10. Kenji has a suitcase, a guitar, and a _____.

GETTING STARTED

Warm Up

1 Look at the picture. Write the number of the person or people.

a. _6_ He's wearing a T-shirt.   **e.** ____ He's wearing jeans.

b. ____ She's wearing a dress.   **f.** ____ He's wearing socks and shoes.

c. ____ She's wearing a sweater.   **g.** ____ They're wearing skirts.

d. ____ He's wearing a jacket and pants.   **h.** ____ She's wearing a shirt.

2 Match the clothes with the colors. Write the correct number.

a. _3_ It's green.   **d.** ____ It's purple.   **g.** ____ It's black and white.

b. ____ They're brown.   **e.** ____ They're orange.   **h.** ____ They're blue.

c. ____ It's pink.   **f.** ____ It's yellow.

3 Work with a partner. Ask and answer questions about the people.

Example:

A: What's she wearing?   **A:** What color is the sweater?

B: She's wearing a sweater.   **B:** It's pink.

4 Work in small groups. Talk about what people in your class are wearing.

Where can I buy some nice shoes?

 5 Listen and read.

A.

SALESPERSON:	Welcome to Style City. Can I help you?
MRS. THOMAS:	Yes. Thank you. I want a shirt for my son. Do you have any boys' shirts?
SALESPERSON:	Yes, we do. These shirts are for boys, and they're on sale.
MRS. THOMAS:	On sale? Great! I like sales!
SALESPERSON:	What color do you want?
MRS. THOMAS:	Blue. My son likes blue.
SALESPERSON:	How about this shirt? Do you like it?
MRS. THOMAS:	Well, I like it, but it has short sleeves. My son likes long sleeves.
SALESPERSON:	Here's one with long sleeves.
MRS. THOMAS:	This one's nice, but it's small. Do you have a large one?
SALESPERSON:	Yes, we do.
MRS. THOMAS:	Great!

B.

MRS. THOMAS:	Do you have any shoes?
SALESPERSON:	I'm sorry. We don't sell shoes.
MRS. THOMAS:	Where can I buy some nice shoes?
SALESPERSON:	Sal's is a good shoe store. It's across from this store.
MRS. THOMAS:	How about videos? I want a video for my daughter. Is there a video store in the mall?
SALESPERSON:	Yes, there is. It's next to this store.
MRS. THOMAS:	Is there a bookstore in the mall, too?
SALESPERSON:	Of course, there's a bookstore. It's across from the video store.
MRS. THOMAS:	And is there a music store?
SALESPERSON:	Yes, it's between the shoe store and the bookstore.
MRS. THOMAS:	Thank you very much. I love this mall!

6 Answer the questions.

a. What does Mrs. Thomas want?

b. Does Mrs. Thomas want a small shirt for her son?

c. Does Mrs. Thomas's son like long sleeves?

d. Does Style City sell shoes?

e. Where can Mrs. Thomas buy shoes?

f. What store is next to Style City?

g. Where is the bookstore in the mall?

h. What store is between the bookstore and the shoe store?

Building Vocabulary
Next to, Between, Across from

next to   between   across from

7   This is Garden State Mall. Read the conversation on page 34 again. Then write the correct names on the stores.

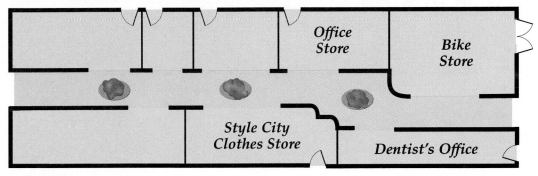

Office Store

Bike Store

Style City Clothes Store

Dentist's Office

8   Look at Garden State Mall. Work with partners. Answer the questions.

Example:

A: Where is Style City?

B: It's next to the video store.

a. What is across from the bike store?

b. What stores is the shoe store between?

c. Where is the office store?

d. What is next to the dentist's office?

e. Where is the bookstore?

Colors

9   Listen and read.

10   Work with a partner. Ask and answer questions about the flags.

red ●	yellow ○	white ○
blue ●	orange ●	black ●
green ●	purple ●	brown ●

Example:

A: What color is Mexico's flag?

B: It's green, white, and red.

Mexico

1. Peru

2. Egypt

3. Japan

4. The Dominican Republic

5. Costa Rica

6. Spain

Stores

11 Listen and read.

12 Work with a partner. Ask and answer questions.

bookstore	clothes store
plant store	music store
shoe store	bike store
video store	

Example:

A: Where can I buy plants?

B: At a plant store.

A: Where can we shop for shoes?

B: At a shoe store.

Days of the Week

	Sunday	Monday	Tuesday	Wednesday	Thursday	Friday	Saturday
A.M.			*English class*		*English class*		*shop*
P.M.		*work at hotel*	*English class*	*work at hotel*	*English class*		*go to theater*

SANDY'S SCHEDULE

13 Work with a partner. Ask and answer questions about Sandy's schedule.

Example:

A: What days does Sandy work?

B: She works on Monday and Wednesday afternoons.

A: Does Sandy have English class on Friday?

B: No, she doesn't.

Talk About It

14 Work with a partner. Complete the chart. Ask and answer questions.

Example:

A: What do you do on Monday afternoons?

B: I go to school. What do you do?

	You	Your Partner
Sunday		
Monday		
Tuesday		
Wednesday		
Thursday		
Friday		
Saturday		

GRAMMAR

Adjectives

We put adjectives before nouns.

	Adjectives	Nouns
Luis has a	**blue**	shirt.
It's an	**interesting**	book.
That's the	**wrong**	color.
This shirt has	**long**	sleeves.
They have	**nice**	shoes.

note Adjectives are always singular in English.

1 Make sentences. Write them on a piece of paper.

Example:

open/store/That/small/is

That small store is open.

a. jacket/want/I/blue/that

b. drives/car/Rodolfo/a/French

c. shoes/Lori/purple/those/likes

d. interesting/have/an/You/family

e. city/This/good/has/schools

f. small/woman/a taxi/That/drives

These/Those

Use *these* for things that are close to you.

Use *those* for things that are not close to you.

Boy: **These** buses are yellow.	**Girl:** **Those** buses are orange.

2 Ask and answer questions about the picture.

Example:

A: What color are these cars?

B: They're red.

A: How about those cars? What color are they?

B: Those cars are green.

Any/Some

We use *any* in questions and in negative sentences. We use *some* in affirmative sentences.

> Do you have **any** large T-shirts?   Yes, I have **some** large T-shirts.
>
> Do you have **any** black shoes?   I don't have **any** black shoes, but I have **some** brown shoes.

3 Complete the conversation with *some* or *any*.

A.

BRENDA: Hello. Do you have **(1.)** _any_ books about bonsai? Bonsai are small trees from Japan.

BOOKSTORE CLERK: Yes. We have **(2.)** _____ books about plants, but we don't have **(3.)** _____ books about Japanese plants. You can look in the video store. They have **(4.)** _____ videos about Japan.

BRENDA: Thank you.

B.

BRENDA: Hello. Do you have **(5.)** _____ videos about bonsai?

VIDEO CLERK: Bonsai? Well, let's see. I have **(6.)** _____ videos about Japanese clothes and Japanese cooking. No, I don't have **(7.)** _____ videos about Japanese trees.

BRENDA: Thanks, but I don't want **(8.)** _____ videos about those things.

VIDEO CLERK: You can look in the library. They have **(9.)** _____ interesting books about plants and trees.

BRENDA: Thanks very much!

4 Work with a partner. Ask and answer questions about Garden State Mall.

Example:

A: Does the shoe store have any running shoes on sale?

B: Yes, it does. It has some running shoes on sale Monday.

A: Does the bike store have any French bikes on sale?

B: No, it doesn't, but it has some Italian bikes on sale.

There is/There are

We use *there is* and *there are* to talk about where something is or is not.

Statements	Yes/No Question	Short Answer
There is a shoe store in the mall.	**Is there** a post office in the mall?	Yes, **there is**. No, **there isn't**.
There are restaurants in the mall.	**Are there** any theaters in the mall?	Yes, **there are**. No, **there aren't**.

note **Contractions:** there is = there's

there is not = there isn't/there's not

5 Work with a partner. Talk about Northland Mall.

Example:

A: Excuse me. Is there a shoe store in Northland Mall?

B: Yes, there is. There's one between the bookstore and the T-shirt store.

A: Thanks.

B: You're welcome.

B: Excuse me. Is there a bike store in the mall?

A: No, there isn't.

B: Thank you.

NORTHLAND MALL
D i r e c t o r y

A   Tim's Books
B   Maple's Shoe Store
C   The T-Shirt Shop
D   Books and Things
E   City Theater
F   Drs. Brown and Sanchez: Dentists
G   Computer City
H   Northland Music
I   First-Class Clothes

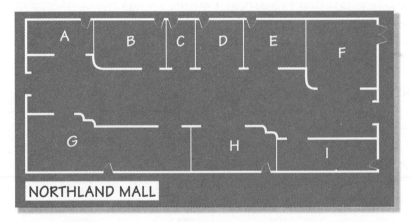

NORTHLAND MALL

6 **Express Yourself** Design your own mall. Draw a map. Use the map on page 35 as an example. Add your favorite stores. Then talk about your mall with a partner. Ask and answer questions.

Example:

A: Are there any shoe stores in your mall?

B: Yes, there are two shoe stores.

A: Where are they?

B: One shoe store is next to the video store. The other is across from the bookstore.

LISTENING and SPEAKING

Listen: The Clothes Designer

STRATEGY **1** **Before You Listen** Do you like designer clothes? Do you know about any clothes designers? What clothes designers do you know about?

2 Listen to the radio interview with a clothes designer. Circle the correct answers.

a.	What is the designer's name?	Nick	Phil	King
b.	What are some colors the designer likes?	orange	yellow	black
c.	What clothes doesn't he like?	pants	shirts	sweaters
d.	Where is he from?	New York	Paris	Tokyo
e.	Where does he work?	New York	Paris	Tokyo

Pronunciation

3 Listen and repeat.

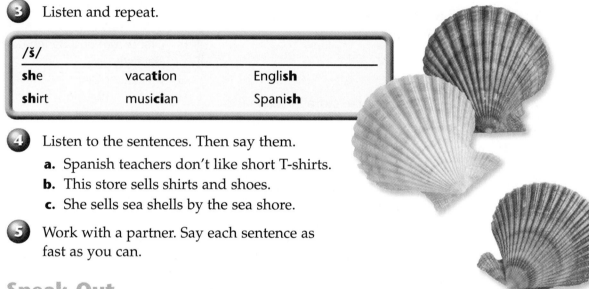

/š/		
she	vaca**ti**on	Engli**sh**
shirt	musi**ci**an	Spani**sh**

4 Listen to the sentences. Then say them.

a. Spanish teachers don't like short T-shirts.
b. This store sells shirts and shoes.
c. She sells sea shells by the sea shore.

5 Work with a partner. Say each sentence as fast as you can.

Speak Out

6 Check (✓) things you like.

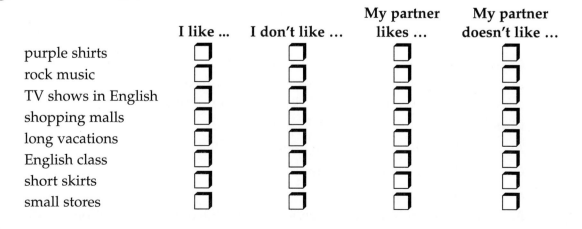

	I like ...	I don't like ...	My partner likes ...	My partner doesn't like ...
purple shirts	☐	☐	☐	☐
rock music	☐	☐	☐	☐
TV shows in English	☐	☐	☐	☐
shopping malls	☐	☐	☐	☐
long vacations	☐	☐	☐	☐
English class	☐	☐	☐	☐
short skirts	☐	☐	☐	☐
small stores	☐	☐	☐	☐

Agreeing and Disagreeing To agree with someone, you can say:

A:	I like malls	**A:**	I don't like malls.
B:	So do I. / Me too.	**B:**	Neither do I. / Me, neither.

To disagree with someone, you can say:

A:	I like rock music.	**A:**	I don't like rock music.
B:	Not me. / I don't.	**B:**	I do.

7 Work with a partner. Complete Exercise 6. Check (✓) the things your partner likes. Agree and disagree.

Example:

A: Do you like purple shirts?

B: No, I don't.

A: Neither do I. Do you like short skirts?

B: Yes, I do.

A: Not me. I like long skirts.

READING and WRITING

Read About It

STRATEGY **1** **Before You Read** Look at the pictures. What can you do in these malls?

2 Read the advertisement.

Something exciting to do in Canada

West Edmonton Mall!

This indoor mall is very, very large. You can shop in 828 stores! You can go to T-shirt stores, music stores, and souvenir stores. You can even buy a car! If you don't want to walk, you can go from store to store in a golf cart. Or you can ride in a rickshaw.

Are you hungry or tired? There are 110 restaurants, from French to Chinese. (If you eat too much in the mall, there are 16 doctors.) Or you can go to the Fantasyland Hotel. It has 120 rooms.

Do you want to have some fun? There are water slides and a roller coaster. Come to West Edmonton Mall with your family and friends.

water slide

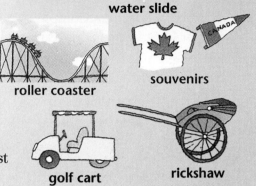
roller coaster
souvenirs
golf cart
rickshaw

3 Correct the sentences. Check your answers with a partner.

Example:
West Edmonton Mall is in ~~the United States~~. *Canada*

a. You can ride from store to store in a car.
b. You can shop in 120 stores.
c. There are 16 restaurants, from French to Chinese.
d. The Fantasyland Hotel has 828 rooms.
e. You can buy a rickshaw at the mall.

Write About It

STRATEGY **4** **Before You Write** Look at your map from Express Yourself on page 39. What stores does your mall have? What can you do at your mall? (You can add more things.)

5 **Write** Work with a partner. Talk about your malls. Do you like your partner's ideas? Choose some ideas you and your partner like. Write an advertisement.

 6 **Check Your Writing** Work with another pair of students. Read each other's advertisements. Correct your sentences. Write the final copy.

- Are your adjectives in the correct place?
- Are *there is* and *there are* correct?
- Is your spelling correct?

OUR HOT DOGS AND HAMBURGERS ARE GREAT!

CAKES

THIRSTY? HAVE A SOFT DRINK

TEA

COFFEE

MILK

SUGAR

PIES

BREAD

PIZZAS

LETTUCE

CHEESE

TOMATOES

ONIONS

MAKE YOUR SALAD HERE!

GETTING STARTED

Warm Up

1. Talk with a partner. What do you want to eat and drink?

Example:

A: I want a salad, but I don't want any onions. What do you want?

B: I'm not hungry. I'm thirsty. I'd like a soft drink, please.

I'd like/I want			
a salad	a piece of cake	some lettuce	a soft drink
a hamburger	some tomatoes	some cheese	some coffee
I don't want			
a hot dog	any sugar	any bread	any milk
a piece of pie	any onions	any tea	

What do we need?

🎧 **2** Listen and read.

A.

MARIO: What do you want to do today?

TONY: Let's go to the mall. I want to buy a book for school.

MARIO: OK. That's a good idea ... Oh, no! I can't go today! Today is my sister's birthday. She's twenty-one years old.

TONY: That's great! So what's the problem?

MARIO: My sister wants a cake for her birthday. Let's make one.

TONY: What! Can you make a cake?

MARIO: Sure. My sister likes chocolate cake, so I make one every year. She says they're great.

TONY: Well, OK. What do we need? Do you have the ingredients ready?

MARIO: Yes, I do. We need some flour, some chocolate, and some sugar. I have them right here. There's some butter and some eggs in the refrigerator. But I don't have any milk.

TONY: Can you make a cake without milk?

MARIO: No. I need to go to the supermarket.

TONY: OK. Let's go buy some milk and make a cake!

INGREDIENTS

flour

eggs

butter

B.

MARIO: Happy birthday, Ellen. Do you like your cake?

ELLEN: It's great, Mario. Thanks!

MARIO: You're welcome, Ellen. But there's one problem.

ELLEN: What's that?

MARIO: Well, every year I make a cake, and every year you eat all of it. I'd like some, too!

ELLEN: I'm so sorry! You can have a piece.

3 Answer the questions.

a. What does Tony want to buy at the mall?

b. Can Mario go to the mall today? Explain.

c. What does Mario's sister like on her birthday?

d. What does Mario need for the cake?

e. Are there any eggs in the refrigerator?

f. What's Mario's sister's name?

g. What's the problem?

h. Can Mario have some cake?

Unit 5

Building Vocabulary

Food

 4 Listen and read.

a. a cheeseburger   **b.** a hot dog with onions   **c.** a salad   **d.** a fried egg with bread and butter

e. a piece of pizza   **f.** some french fries   **g.** some fried chicken   **h.** a cheese sandwich with tomatoes

5 Work with a partner. Look at the pictures. Tell your partner what you want.

Example:

A: What do you want?

B: I'd like a cheese sandwich with tomatoes, please.

Months

6 Listen and read.

January						
m	t	w	t	f	s	s
					1	2
3	4	5	6	7	8	9
10	11	12	13	14	15	16
17	18	19	20	21	22	23
24	25	26	27	28	29	30
31						

February						
m	t	w	t	f	s	s
1	2	3	4	5	6	7
8	9	10	11	12	13	14
15	16	17	18	19	20	21
22	23	24	25	26	27	28
29						

March						
m	t	w	t	f	s	s
		1	2	3	4	5
	8	9	10	11	12	
15	16	17	18	19		
22	23	24	25	26		
29	30	31				

April						
m	t	w	t	f	s	s
					1	2
	4	5	6	7	8	9
	11	12	13	14	15	16
	17	18	19	20	21	22	23
	24	25	26	27	28	29	30

May						
m	t	w	t	f	s	s
	2	3	4	5	6	7
	9	10	11	12	13	14
	16	17	18	19	20	21
	23	24	25	26	27	28
	30	31				

June						
m	t	w	t	f	s	s
				1	2	3	4
7	8	9	10	11		
14	15	16	17	18		
19	20	21	22	23	24	25
26	27	28	29	30		

July						
m	t	w	t	f	s	s
					1	2
3	4	5	6	7	8	9
10	11	12	13	14	15	16
17	18	19	20	21	22	23
24	25	26	27	28	29	30
31						

August						
m	t	w	t	f	s	s
	1	2	3	4	5	6
8	9	10	11	12	13	
15	16	17	18	19	20	
22	23	24	25	26	27	
29	30	31				

September						
m	t	w	t	f	s	s
		1	2	3		
6	7	8	9	10		
13	14	15	16	17		
20	21	22	23	24		
27	28	29	30			

October						
m	t	w	t	f	s	s
						1
3	4	5	6	7	8	
9	10	11	12	13	14	15
16	17	18	19	20	21	22
23	24	25	26	27	28	29
30	31					

November						
m	t	w	t	f	s	s
1	2	3	4	5		
7	8	9	10	11	12	
14	15	16	17	18	19	
21	22	23	24	25	26	
28	29	30				

December						
m	t	w	t	f	s	s
		1	2	3		
5	6	7	8	9	10	
12	13	14	15	16	17	
19	20	21	22	23	24	
26	27	28	29	30	31	

Talk About It

7   **a.** Ask your classmates about their birthdays. Write their names next to the correct months in the calendar.

Example:

ALICIA: When's your birthday?   **ALICIA:** How old are you?

PABLO: It's in March.   **PABLO:** I'm sixteen.

b. Make a graph of your classmates' birthdays.

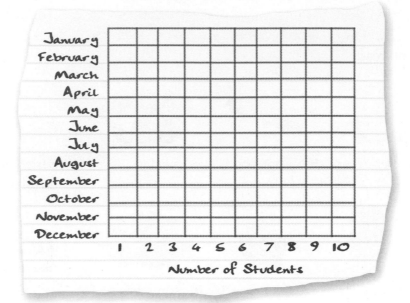

GRAMMAR

Count Nouns

We can use *a* or *an* before singular count nouns. Plural count nouns usually end in *–s* or *–es*.

Singular	Plural	
a hamburger	hamburger**s**	I'd like **a** hamburger, please.
an egg	egg**s**	He likes egg**s**.
a tomato	tomato**es**	They don't want tomato**es** in their salad.

Non-count Nouns

We cannot use *a* or *an* with non-count nouns. Non-count nouns do not usually have plural forms. We can use *some* or *any* with non-count nouns.

I'd like **some** sugar.	There isn't **any** coffee.
I don't want **any** lettuce.	Do you want **any** milk?

We can use some expressions to talk about non-count nouns.

I'd like **a glass of** milk.	I need to buy **a head of** lettuce.
We want **two cups of** coffee, please.	They want **three pieces of** cake.

1 Write *a, an, some, any,* or X (for no word) on the line.

WAITER: What can I get for you?

MAX: I'm hungry! I'd like **(1.)** _____ salad and **(2.)** _____ small pizza with **(3.)** _____ onions.

JACOB: Can I have **(4.)** _____ hamburger, please? I'd like **(5.)** _____ lettuce on it, but I don't want **(6.)** _____ tomatoes. I don't like **(7.)** _____ tomatoes.

WAITER: What do you want to drink?

MAX: I'd like **(8.)** _____ coffee, please.

WAITER: Do you want **(9.)** _____ milk with that?

MAX: No, thanks. But I'd like **(10.)** _____ sugar.

JACOB: I don't want **(11.)** _____ coffee, thanks. I'd like **(12.)** _____ tea with **(13.)** _____ milk and **(14.)** _____ piece of chocolate cake.

Possessive Adjectives

Possessive adjectives come before nouns.

I like **my** sandwich.	It likes **its** food.
You need **your** jacket.	You need **your** books.
He has **his** briefcase.	We need **our** sweaters.
She likes **her** backpack.	They want **their** drinks.

 Possessive adjectives do not change with plural nouns.

I like **my** friend.   I like **my** friends.

We like **their** idea.   We like **their** ideas.

2 Write the correct possessive adjective.

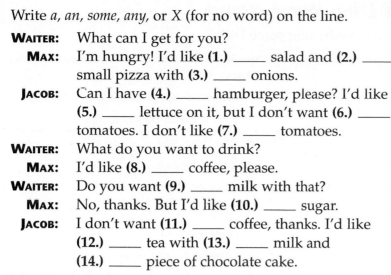

I'm seventeen years old. Today is **(1.)** _____ birthday.
This is my brother. **(2.)** _____ birthday is in June.
That's **(3.)** _____ sister. **(4.)** _____ birthday is in October.

GEORGE: We need a ride to the theater. Where's **(5.)** _____ taxi?

TAXI DRIVER: Next to the bus. It's the one with **(6.)** _____ door open.

GEORGE: Can **(7.)** _____ guitars go in **(8.)** _____ taxi? And what about our friends? Can **(9.)** _____ drums go in **(10.)** _____ taxi?

TAXI DRIVER: Yes. You and **(11.)** _____ guitars and **(12.)** _____ friends and **(13.)** _____ drums can go in **(14.)** _____ taxi. Let's go!

Infinitives with *Like, Want, Need*

We can use an infinitive (*to* + verb) after some verbs.

I **like to eat** hamburgers.	I **don't like to eat** hot dogs.
Mary **wants to buy** some milk.	She **doesn't want to buy** any cheese.
I **need to study**.	We **don't need to go** to the mall.
Does she **need to go** home?	Yes, she does./No, she doesn't.
Do you **want to have** coffee?	Yes, I do./No, I don't.
Do they **like to dance**?	Yes, they do./No, they don't.
What does he **like to do**?	He **likes to swim**.
What do we **need to buy**?	We **need to buy** some lettuce.
When do they **want to eat**?	They **want to eat** now.

3 What do you like to do? Write three things on a piece of paper. What don't you like to do? Write three things.

4 Talk to your classmates. Find someone who likes to do what you like to do and someone who doesn't like to do what you don't like to do.

Example:

A: Do you like to swim?

B: Yes, I do. Do you like to make cakes?

A: No, I don't. I don't like to cook.

B: What do you like to do?

A: I like to make clothes.

Let's

We can make suggestions with *let's*.

Let's	eat.
	go to the theater.
	listen to some music.

5 Match the sentences and suggestions. Write the correct letter on the line.

1. _____ I can't walk to school.
2. _____ I'm hungry.
3. _____ I need a new jacket.
4. _____ I'm cold.
5. _____ I like Latin music.
6. _____ I have a problem.
7. _____ I need to buy some food.
8. _____ I'm thirsty.
9. _____ It's 10:00 p.m.
10. _____ It's my birthday tomorrow.

a. Let's listen to a Ricky Martin tape.
b. Let's talk about it.
c. Let's close the window.
d. Let's buy some soft drinks.
e. Let's take a bus.
f. Let's have a party.
g. Let's go to the mall.
h. Let's go to the supermarket.
i. Let's make sandwiches.
j. Let's go home.

6 **Express Yourself** Work in groups of three. **A** is a waiter, **B** and **C** are customers. Look at the menu. Talk about what you want to eat and drink. Make suggestions. Tell the waiter what you like.

Example:

A: What can I get for you?

B: I'd like a chicken sandwich and a cup of coffee, please.

C: I want a cheeseburger. Let's have some french fries.

B: Good idea.

A: Would you like any dessert?

C: Let's have some apple pie.

B: Oh, yes!!

Grand Mall Menu

FOOD
HAMBURGER
CHEESEBURGER
HOT DOG
CHICKEN SANDWICH
SALAD
FRENCH FRIES

DRINKS
COFFEE
TEA
ORANGE JUICE
MILK

DESSERT
CHOCOLATE CAKE
APPLE PIE
CHEESECAKE

LISTENING and SPEAKING

Listen: At the Pizza Restaurant

STRATEGY **1** **Before You Listen** Look at the pictures. Describe the food. Are the pizzas large or small? What's on them? What's in the salads?

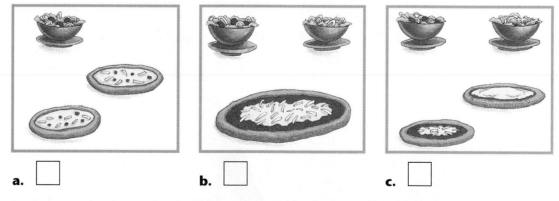

a. [ ] b. [ ] c. [ ]

 2 Ed is at work. He works at Pizza Connection. Look at the pictures in Exercise 1 and listen to the telephone conversations. Write the number of the conversation in the box next to the correct picture.

Pronunciation

3 Listen and repeat.

/h/			
a. hand and	**c.** heat eat	**e.** howl owl
b. his is	**d.** hi I	**f.** ham am

4 Listen. Circle the word you hear.

a. hand   and   **c.** heat   eat   **e.** howl   owl
b. his   is   **d.** hi   I   **f.** ham   am

Speak Out

STRATEGY ▶ **Asking a Question Politely** To ask a question politely, you can say:

Excuse me. Do you (drink tea with milk)?

5 Walk around the classroom. Ask questions politely. When someone answers *yes*, write his or her name on the line. Add your own ideas.

1. _____ drinks tea with milk.

2. _____ likes to drink milk.

3. _____ eats some chocolate every day.

4. _____ has a salad every day.

5. _____ likes chocolate cake.

6. _____ likes to eat eggs in the morning.

7. _____ likes tomatoes.

8. _____ needs to drink coffee in the morning.

9. _____

10. _____

READING and WRITING

Read About It

STRATEGY **1** **Before You Read** Look at the picture and the title of the reading. What is the reading about? Where is it from?

★ ★ ★ **CHICAGO STAR** ★ ★ ★

TASTE OF CHICAGO

The Windy City's Food Festival

Every year the city of Chicago has an outdoor food festival. It's called *Taste of Chicago*. For eight days you can't drive a car on Columbus Drive or Congress Drive. These two big streets in downtown Chicago are closed for the festival. But you can walk, eat, and listen to music. The festival is open in the morning, afternoon, and evening. About 375,000 people go there every day.

There is food from over eighty different Chicago restaurants at the festival. For example, you can eat quesadillas—a kind of round, flat bread (or tortilla) filled with meat or vegetables and cheese—in a Mexican restaurant. Then you can have tempura—shrimp and vegetables in flour and fried in oil—in a Japanese restaurant. And you can have shish kebab—pieces of meat and vegetables cooked over a fire on skewers (long, thin pieces of wood or metal)—in a Turkish restaurant. Of course, there is a lot of American food, too—hamburgers, hot dogs, and fried chicken.

How much do people usually eat? Here are some interesting numbers: 55,000 hot dogs, 460,000 slices of pizza, 50,000 slices of cake, 102,000 Chinese egg rolls, and 27,000 kilos of french fries.

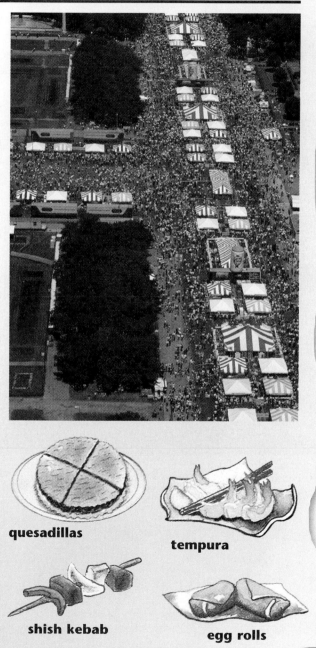

quesadillas

tempura

shish kebab

egg rolls

Match the words. Write the correct letter.

1. _____ The Windy City   **a.** round, flat bread
2. _____ egg rolls   **b.** Turkish food
3. _____ hamburgers   **c.** Chicago
4. _____ quesadillas   **d.** Japanese food
5. _____ shish kebab   **e.** long, thin pieces of wood or metal
6. _____ tempura   **f.** Chinese food
7. _____ tortilla   **g.** American food
8. _____ skewers   **h.** Mexican food

Write About It

STRATEGY

3 **Before You Write** Are there any special food festivals in your city or town? What special kinds of food does your city have? Work with a partner. Make a list of these festivals and foods.

4 **Write** With a partner, write a short newspaper article about a food festival. You can also write about a special kind of food in your city.

If you write about a food festival, answer these questions:

- When is the festival?
- How many days or nights is it?
- What things can you do? (Can you listen to music?)
- How many people usually go to the festival?
- What kinds of food can you eat there?

Use the article about Chicago as a model.

If you write about a special food, answer these questions:

- What is the name of the food?
- Where can you eat this food?
- How do you make it?
- Where is the best restaurant to eat this food?

5 **Check Your Writing** Work with another pair of students. Read each other's articles. Correct your articles. Write the final copy.

- Are your count and non-count nouns correct?
- Are your verbs correct?
- Is your spelling correct?

GETTING STARTED

Warm Up

1 Look at the pictures. Write the correct letter.

—— **1.** woman; getting a magazine
—— **2.** reporter; following a man
—— **3.** taxi driver; stopping behind some motorcycles
—— **4.** girl; standing in front of a bookstore
—— **5.** person; reading a newspaper
—— **6.** boy and girl; waiting for the bus
—— **7.** men; getting off their motorcycles
—— **8.** spies; taking pictures

2 Work with a partner. Ask and answer questions about the people.

Example:

A: What is the person in picture B doing?

B: She's getting a magazine.

Where are they going?

3 Listen and read.

Mr. Hanson is a reporter for *Today's Spy* magazine, and Mrs. Hanson writes spy stories. They aren't working today, but they're thinking about spies.

MR. HANSON: What are you doing, honey?

MRS. HANSON: I'm waiting for the mail carrier. What time is it?

MR. HANSON: It's a quarter after three.

MRS. HANSON: That's strange. He comes at three o'clock every day. Where do you think he is? I'm waiting for a very important letter.

MR. HANSON: Look, honey. There he is.

MRS. HANSON: That's not the mail carrier. That's our neighbor, Mr. Everet. That's strange! He's just sitting in his car reading the newspaper.

MR. HANSON: Is he waiting for his wife?

MRS. HANSON: His wife's at work now!

MR. HANSON: Look! A person on a motorcycle is stopping behind Mr. Everet's car.

MRS. HANSON: It's a woman, but it's not Mr. Everet's wife! Who do you think she is?

MR. HANSON: I don't know. Look! She's getting off her motorcycle, and she's talking to Mr. Everet.

MRS. HANSON: Yes, but he isn't talking. He's just listening.

MR. HANSON: Hmm. That's interesting. Now Mr. Everet and the woman are getting on the motorcycle. She's carrying his briefcase, and he's driving! Where are they going? This is all very strange. Let's follow those two.

MRS. HANSON: OK. Let's get our cameras! I need my glasses for this. My glasses … Where are my glasses?

MR. HANSON: You're wearing them!

MRS. HANSON: Oh!!

4 Answer the questions.

a. What do Mr. and Mrs. Hanson do?

b. What are they doing now?

c. What time is it?

d. Who is Mr. Everet?

e. Is Mr. Everet waiting for his wife?

f. Where is Mr. Everet's wife?

g. What is the woman riding?

h. What do Mr. and Mrs. Hanson want to do?

5 Look at the picture. Complete the sentences with words from the box.

| behind |
| carrying |
| glasses |
| in front of |
| magazine |
| motorcycle |
| park |
| taking |

a. These people are in the _____.

b. Mr. and Mrs. Hanson are _____ the car.

c. Mr. Hanson is _____ a picture.

d. The strange woman is _____ a briefcase.

e. She and Mr. Everet are on a _____.

f. Mr. Everet is _____ the woman.

Building Vocabulary

Time

🎧 **6** Look at the clocks. Listen.
What time is it?

a. It's a quarter to three.

b. It's ten to three.

c. It's three o'clock.

d. It's five after three.

e. It's a quarter after three.

f. It's three-thirty.

7 Work with a partner. Ask and tell the time.

Example:

A: What time is it?

B: It's ten to three.

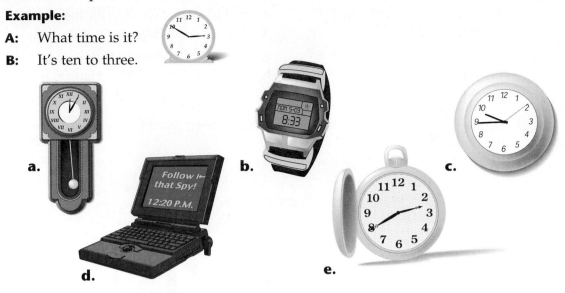

a.   b.   c.

d.   e.

Talk About It

8 Work with a partner. Ask and answer questions about what time you do things each day. Use the expressions in the box and your own ideas.

watch TV	meet your friends
eat	go home
go to school	listen to music

Example:

A: What time do you go to school?

B: I go to school at 8:30.

GRAMMAR

Present Progressive Tense

We use the present progressive tense (*be* + verb + *–ing*) to talk about activities that are happening now.

Affirmative	Negative
I'**m waiting** for the mail carrier.	I'**m not reading** the newspaper.
Mr. Everet **is sitting** in his car.	He **isn't driving**./He'**s not driving**.
She'**s talking** to Mr. Everet.	She **isn't listening**./She'**s not listening**.
They'**re getting** their cameras.	They **aren't carrying** briefcases./They'**re not carrying** briefcases.

note   drive + ing = driving   sit + ing = sitting   run + ing = running
ride + ing = riding   get + ing = getting

Work with a partner. Look at the pictures on page 53. Make a sentence about a person or some people in the pictures. Can your partner guess who you are talking about?

Example:

A: This person is standing in front of the bookstore.

B: Is it the person in picture A?

A: Yes, it is.

Present Progressive Tense: Yes/No Questions

In yes/no questions, we use *be* + subject + verb + *–ing*.

Yes/No Questions	Short Answers
Are you **waiting** for an important letter?	Yes, I **am**.
Is Mr. Everet **driving** a car?	No, he **isn't**./No, he**'s not**.
Is the woman **riding** a motorcycle?	Yes, she **is**.
Are Mr. and Mrs. Hanson **carrying** briefcases?	No, they **aren't**./No, they**'re not**.
Are they **getting** their cameras?	Yes, they **are**.

2 Look at the picture on page 55. Read the answers. Write yes/no questions.

1. A: _____?
    B: No, Mr. and Mrs. Hanson aren't working today.

2. A: _____?
    B: No, they aren't shopping. They're following Mr. Everet.

3. A: _____?
    B: Yes, he's taking pictures.

4. A: _____?
    B: No, Mr. Everet isn't walking. He's riding a motorcycle.

5. A: _____?
    B: Yes, a woman is riding with Mr. Everet.

3 Work with a partner. Take turns. Make statements about people in the class. Ask yes/no questions.

Example:

A: This person is wearing black pants.

B: Is it a man?

A: Yes, it is.

B: Is he sitting next to Carlos?

A: Yes, he is.

B: Is he Luis?

A: Yes, he is.

Present Progressive Tense: Information Questions

Questions	Possible Answers
What are you **doing**?	I**'m waiting for** an important letter.
What is Mr. Everet **reading**?	He**'s reading** a newspaper.
Who is riding a motorcycle?	A woman **is riding** a motorcycle.
Who is she **riding with**?	She**'s riding with** Mr. Everet.
Where are they **going**?	They**'re going to** the park.

4 Look at the picture. Work with a partner. Ask and answer information questions about Beth and Mary.

Example:

A: What's Mary doing?

B: She's riding a bike.

A: Who is Mary riding with?

B: Beth.

Beth   **Mary**

5 Work with a partner. Ask and answer questions about each sentence. Use *what*, *where*, or *who*.

Example:

Barbara is drinking some coffee with her mother at a restaurant.

A: Who is drinking coffee?	A: Who's she drinking the coffee with?
B: Barbara.	B: Her mother.
A: What's Barbara drinking?	A: Where are they drinking coffee?
B: Some coffee.	B: At a restaurant.

a. The reporter is following the spy at the airport.

b. Mrs. Hanson is writing a new spy story for a magazine.

c. My brothers are buying new glasses at the mall.

d. The mail carrier is carrying a letter to my neighbor.

e. Tony and Mario are making a birthday cake for Maria.

f. Mr. Hanson is taking pictures of Mr. Everet in the park.

6 **Express Yourself** Write six sentences on a piece of paper. Use the present progressive tense.

Then work with a partner. Take turns. Read one of your sentences. Your partner makes a question for your sentence. If your partner asks a correct question, he or she gets 1 point. How many correct questions can you ask?

Example:

A: Mr. Gonzalez is writing on the chalkboard.

B: Who is writing on the chalkboard?

A: That's correct. You get 1 point. Read one of your sentences.

LISTENING and SPEAKING

Listen: What's Happening Now?

STRATEGY **1** **Before You Listen** Look at the pictures. Who are the people? What is happening in each picture?

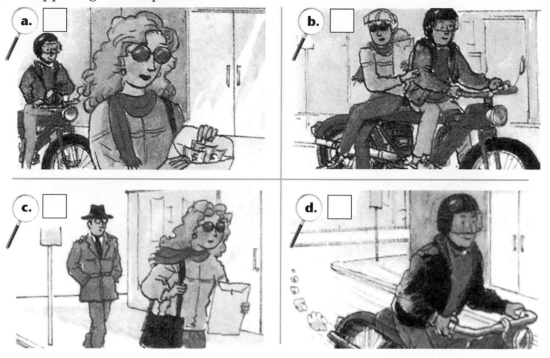

a. ☐   b. ☐   c. ☐   d. ☐

2 Mr. and Mrs. Hanson are watching Mr. Everet and a woman. Listen to the conversation and number the pictures from 1–4 in the correct order.

Pronunciation

3 Listen and repeat.

/n/ and /ŋ/	
/n/	**/ŋ/**
wi**n**	wi**ng**
thi**n**	thi**ng**
si**n**	si**ng**

4 Listen to each word. Check the correct sound.

	/n/	/ŋ/		/n/	/ŋ/		/n/	/ŋ/
a.	☐	☐	d.	☐	☐	g.	☐	☐
b.	☐	☐	e.	☐	☐	h.	☐	☐
c.	☐	☐	f.	☐	☐	i.	☐	☐

Speak Out

 Work with a partner. One person looks at Picture A. The other person looks at Picture B on the bottom of page 62. Find five differences. You can ask only yes/no questions.

Picture A

Example:

A: Is a boy playing a guitar in your picture?

B: Yes.

A: Does he have brown hair?

B: No, he doesn't.

STRATEGY **Checking Information** To check your five differences, you can say:

> **A:** Difference number one is the boy's hair. In my picture, the boy has brown hair.
>
> **B:** That's right. In my picture, the boy has black hair. Difference number two is …

READING and WRITING

Read About It

1 **Before You Read** Mr. Hanson has pictures of Mr. Everet. Mrs. Hanson has pictures of the strange man and the strange woman. Look at the pictures on page 61. What's happening?

2 Read the sentences. Write the letter of the correct sentence in the box.

a. The man and woman are talking to a salesperson. The woman is carrying an envelope.

b. The man and woman are looking at bikes. They have an envelope with money.

c. Mrs. Everet is riding a motorcycle. She likes it. Mr. Everet and their daughter are watching.

d. The man and woman are walking out of the store. She has a blue bike and he has a red bike.

e. Mr. Everet and his family are in the park. They are eating a birthday cake. Today is Mrs. Everet's birthday. There is a motorcycle behind the tree. It's for Mrs. Everet.

 3 Answer the questions.

a. Who is the woman in picture 1?

b. What is the Everet family doing in the park?

c. What is today?

d. Who is riding the motorcycle?

e. Is the motorcycle new?

f. Where are the strange woman and man in Mrs. Hanson's pictures?

g. What are they doing there?

4 Discuss these questions with a partner. Tell the class your answers.

a. Do you think the strange man, the strange woman, and Mr. Everet are spies? Explain.

b. Who do you think the strange man is?

c. What is the woman doing with the money?

d. What is Mrs. Everet getting for her birthday?

Mr. Hanson's pictures

Mrs. Hanson's pictures

Write About It

 STRATEGY

5 **Before You Write** Work with a partner. Talk about the picture. Where are the things and the people in the picture? Who are the people? What are they doing? What are they wearing? What colors are their clothes? Talk about your ideas.

6 **Write** Use your ideas from Exercise 5. Write eight sentences about the picture on a piece of paper.

Example:

A white dog is sitting in front of a big red truck. A man is standing next to the truck. He is wearing white clothes. He is talking to the dog.

 7 **Check Your Writing** Work with a partner. Read your partner's sentences. Correct your sentences. Write the final copy.

- Are *there is* and *there are* correct?
- Are the present progressive verbs correct?
- Is the spelling correct?

Picture B

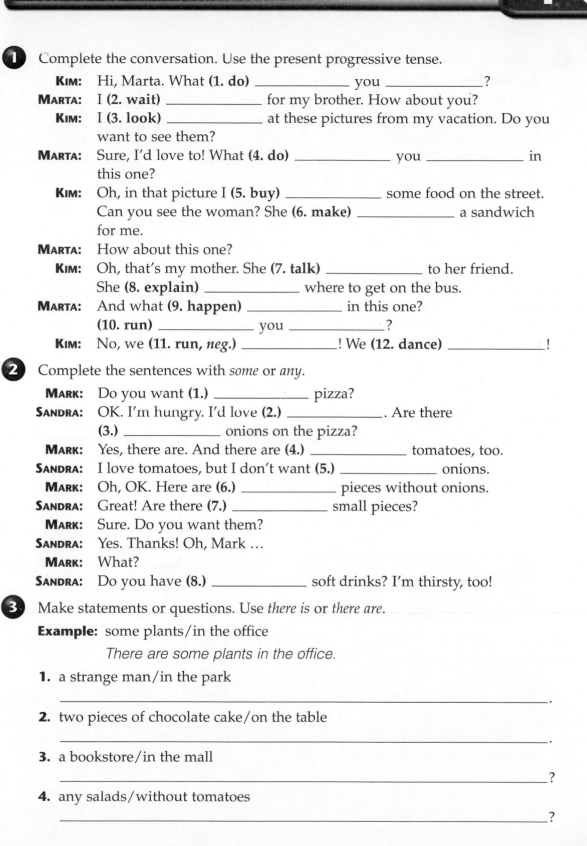

1 Complete the conversation. Use the present progressive tense.

KIM: Hi, Marta. What **(1. do)** _____ you _____?

MARTA: I **(2. wait)** _____ for my brother. How about you?

KIM: I **(3. look)** _____ at these pictures from my vacation. Do you want to see them?

MARTA: Sure, I'd love to! What **(4. do)** _____ you _____ in this one?

KIM: Oh, in that picture I **(5. buy)** _____ some food on the street. Can you see the woman? She **(6. make)** _____ a sandwich for me.

MARTA: How about this one?

KIM: Oh, that's my mother. She **(7. talk)** _____ to her friend. She **(8. explain)** _____ where to get on the bus.

MARTA: And what **(9. happen)** _____ in this one? **(10. run)** _____ you _____?

KIM: No, we **(11. run, neg.)** _____! We **(12. dance)** _____!

2 Complete the sentences with *some* or *any*.

MARK: Do you want **(1.)** _____ pizza?

SANDRA: OK. I'm hungry. I'd love **(2.)** _____. Are there **(3.)** _____ onions on the pizza?

MARK: Yes, there are. And there are **(4.)** _____ tomatoes, too.

SANDRA: I love tomatoes, but I don't want **(5.)** _____ onions.

MARK: Oh, OK. Here are **(6.)** _____ pieces without onions.

SANDRA: Great! Are there **(7.)** _____ small pieces?

MARK: Sure. Do you want them?

SANDRA: Yes. Thanks! Oh, Mark …

MARK: What?

SANDRA: Do you have **(8.)** _____ soft drinks? I'm thirsty, too!

3 Make statements or questions. Use *there is* or *there are*.

Example: some plants/in the office

There are some plants in the office.

1. a strange man/in the park

_____.

2. two pieces of chocolate cake/on the table

_____.

3. a bookstore/in the mall

_____?

4. any salads/without tomatoes

_____?

4 Complete the conversations with the words from the box.

I	we	her
you	they	its
he	my	our
she	your	their
it	his	

A. ROBERTO: Where's Katie?

MARCO: (1.) _____'s shopping.

ROBERTO: Did she go with (2.) _____ boyfriend?

MARCO: (3.) _____ think so.

B. ELENA: Excuse me. I think (4.) _____ are wearing (5.) _____ sweater.

PIA: No, Elena. (6.) _____ sweater is on that desk near the door.

ELENA: How strange! (7.) _____ wasn't there this morning. Thanks!

C. ALI: What are (8.) _____ doing Carlos?

CARLOS: (9.) _____'m waiting for (10.) _____ friends, Yoko, Anna, and Sami.

ALI: Where are (11.) _____?

CARLOS: (12.) _____'re eating lunch at the restaurant.

Vocabulary Review

Complete the reading with words and expressions from the box.

salesperson	new
across from	restaurant
on sale	between
every	neighbor
schedule	week
motorcycle	problem

Roman is my (1.) _____. He rides his (2.) _____ to work (3.) _____ day. Here is his (4.) _____: on Monday, Tuesday, and Wednesday mornings he works at the hospital; on Thursday and Friday afternoons he works in a (5.) _____.

When Roman isn't working, he goes to the bookstore. The bookstore is (6.) _____ the hospital. It's (7.) _____ Marty's shoe store and the plant store. Roman's friend, Rebecca, is a (8.) _____ there. She tells Roman about all the (9.) _____ books (10.) _____. Roman buys books every (11.) _____.

Roman has one (12.) _____. He works all week. He has no time to read the books he buys.

LET'S GET IN SHAPE!

1.
2.
3.
4.
5.
6.
7.
8.

GETTING STARTED

Warm Up

1 What can you do at a health club? Look at the pictures. Write the numbers.

- **a.** _____ swim
- **b.** _____ run
- **c.** _____ walk
- **d.** _____ exercise
- **e.** _____ jump rope
- **f.** _____ ride exercise bikes
- **g.** _____ play basketball
- **h.** _____ use body-building machines

2 Work with a partner. What does your partner like to do? What do you like to do? Ask and answer questions.

Example:

A: Do you like to swim?

B: No, I don't. Do you?

A: Yes, I do. I also like to play basketball.

B: Me, too, but I don't like to jump rope.

A: Me, neither.

How often do you come to the health club?

3 Listen and read.

A.

SUE: Alana, look at this ad. The health club wants new members. They're having an open house tonight.

ALANA: I don't need a health club. I'm not out of shape and I'm also very healthy. I exercise every day, and I don't have the time or the money to go to a health club.

SUE: Me, neither. But let's go and look. Come on! We can have fun, and we don't need any money. What are you doing tonight?

ALANA: You know I'm not doing anything. OK. Let's go.

B.

TOM: Hi. I'm Tom. I work here at the New You Fitness Club. This is our weight room. Stan and his wife Antonia are over there lifting weights. They're in great shape. They lift weights every evening. Do you like to lift weights, Sue?

SUE: No, I don't. It's very hard.

TOM: What kind of exercise do you usually like to do, Alana?

ALANA: Well, I like to watch Kathy Turner's exercise show on TV. I exercise with her every day, and I also like to ride my bike. It's fun and easy.

C.

TOM: Well, this is the big exercise room. There are exercise classes here all day. We have a lot of exercise bikes and body-building machines.

SUE: I don't know how to use body-building machines.

TOM: No problem. I can teach you. And here is the swimming pool.

SUE: Look Alana, there's Julia Bradley. She's swimming in the pool.

TOM: Yes, Julia's a new member. Do you like to play basketball? Julia and her friends play basketball here every week.

ALANA: Really? I love to play basketball.

D.

TOM: Here's the health-food bar. You can have breakfast, lunch, dinner, or a snack here. You can see that a lot of members are sitting at the bar now.

SUE: Hey, isn't that Ted Crampton?

TED: Hi, Sue! Hi, Alana! Don't you think this health club is great? Do you want a drink? They have juice—orange, apple, or grape—and water, of course!

SUE: Yes, I'd like some apple juice. Thanks! How often do you come to the health club, Ted?

TED: Oh, I come every day! I like it here.

SUE: Me, too! What do you think, Alana?

ALANA: It's great! Good-bye TV and hello New You!

Health food bar

4 Answer the questions.

1. What does Sue want to do?
2. What kind of exercise does Alana like?
3. What do Alana and Sue see at the health club?
4. Who do Alana and Sue know at the health club?
5. What doesn't Sue know how to do?
6. What is Ted Crampton doing?
7. What can you do at the New You Fitness Club?

Building Vocabulary

Meals

breakfast

lunch

dinner

snack

5 Do you eat healthy food? Write what you eat.

Breakfast _____

Lunch _____

Dinner _____

Snack _____

Expressions with *Have*

We can use *have* in expressions. We can use the simple present or the present progressive tense with these expressions.

I **have a good time** every day at the health club.	I'm **having a good time** today.
We don't **have fun** at work.	We're **not having fun** at work today.
William **has lunch** every day at 12:30.	It's 12:30. William is **having lunch** now.
They **have eggs** for breakfast.	They're **having eggs** for breakfast.
We don't **have time** or **money** to go on vacation.*	

note * Some expressions with *have* cannot be used in the present progressive tense.

6 Work with a partner. Ask and answer questions.

Example:

a. Do you have a large family? How many brothers and sisters do you have?

b. What do you like to have for lunch? for breakfast? for dinner?

c. Are you having fun in class today?

d. Do you have time to join a health club?

e. Do you have a good time with your friends?

Talk About It

7 Work in groups of three. Complete the chart for your group.

Example:

A: What do you have for breakfast?

B: I have eggs, bread, and milk. How about you?

A: I don't eat eggs. I have bread with butter and coffee for breakfast.

Name	Breakfast	Lunch	Dinner	Snacks

GRAMMAR

The Simple Present Tense: *How often, Every*

We use *how often* and *every* to talk about activities we do on a schedule.

How often does Ted go to the health club?	He goes there **every day**.
How often does Alana ride her bike?	She rides her bike **every Saturday**.
How often do Julia's friends play basketball?	They play basketball **every week**.

1 Write five sentences about yourself. Use *every*.

Example:

I go to English class every day.

1. _____ .
2. _____ .
3. _____ .
4. _____ .
5. _____ .

2 Work with a partner. Find out what your partner likes to do. Ask and answer questions.

Example:

A: What do you like to do?

B: I like to ride my bike.

A: How often do you ride your bike?

B: I ride it every day.

Simple Present Tense vs. Present Progressive Tense

We use the simple present tense to talk about everyday activities. We use the present progressive tense to talk about activities that are happening now.

	Questions	Answers
Simple Present	What **do** you **do** on Sunday morning?	I **ride** my bike.
	Do you **ride** your bike every Sunday?	Yes, I **do**.
Present Progressive	It's 3:00. What **is** Debbie **doing** now?	She**'s riding** her bike.
	Is she **riding** in the park?	Yes, she **is**.

note

Everyday activities:
in the afternoon
on Saturday
every week

Activities happening now:
this afternoon
today
now

3 Look at Yoko's schedule. Work with a partner. Ask and answer the questions.

Yoko's Afternoon Schedule						
Sunday	**Monday**	**Tuesday**	**Wednesday**	**Thursday**	**Friday**	**Saturday**
read	do English homework	swim	work in father's office	do English homework	bake a cake	go to the park with friends

    a. What does Yoko do every Friday afternoon?
    b. When does Yoko do her English homework?
    c. Where does Yoko work every Wednesday afternoon?
    d. When does Yoko swim?
    e. What do Yoko and her friends do every Saturday afternoon?
    f. It's Tuesday afternoon. What is Yoko doing?
    g. Yoko is baking a cake now. What day is it?
    h. It's Sunday afternoon. What is Yoko doing?

Non-action Verbs

Some verbs do not describe actions or activities. We usually do not use these verbs in the present progressive tense.

know	need	want	like	love	have	be

4 Complete the story. Use the non-action verbs in the box.

    Sue **(1.)** ___wants___ to get in shape. She **(2.)** _____ the time to work out. She **(3. *neg.*)** _____ to lift weights, but she **(4.)** _____ to swim. She **(5.)** _____ the health club **(6.)** _____ new members. A lot of her friends **(7.)** _____ members, but Sue **(8. *neg.*)** _____ . Sue **(9.)** _____ to join the club, but she **(10. *neg.*)** _____ the money.

Imperatives

We use imperatives to tell people what to do and what not to do. (The subject is always *you*, but we don't say it or write it.)

Affirmative	**Negative**
Run.	**Don't** stop!
Go.	
Listen.	**Don't** talk, please.
Sit down.	
Repeat.	
Close your book.	**Don't** open your book!

Run!

5 Express Yourself Work with a partner. Read the sentences. Who is talking? Who are they talking to? Use words in the box. Different answers are possible.

a clerk	a mother
a daughter	a musician
a doctor	a son
a father	a student
a friend	a teacher

Example:

A: Eat a lot of fruit!

B: A mother is talking to her son.

a. Eat your dinner!

b. Don't wear that short skirt!

c. Don't play my guitar!

d. Fill in the form, please.

e. Don't buy an old car.

f. Don't eat my snack.

g. Exercise every day!

h. Don't write in the book!

i. Have a good vacation.

j. Write your answers on a piece of paper.

k. Have a good time.

l. Idea of your own

LISTENING and SPEAKING

Listen: The New Health Club Member

 1 Before You Listen Look at the pictures. Where are these people? What do you think they are doing?

1. _____

2. _____

3. _____

4. _____

5. _____

2 Listen to the conversation. What are the office workers doing now? Write each name under the correct picture in Exercise 1.

Richard	Harold
Sandra	Tony
Luis	Brian
Mona	

Pronunciation

 3 Listen and repeat.

/l/	and	/r/
light		**r**ight
lead		**r**ead
lane		**r**ain
lake		**r**ake

 4 Listen to each word. Circle the correct sound.

1. l r	**3.** l r	**5.** l r	**7.** l r
2. l r	**4.** l r	**6.** l r	**8.** l r

Speak Out

STRATEGY **Getting More Information** When you want more information, you can say:

> Can you tell me more?/Please tell me more.
> Can you explain?/Please explain.

5 Work with a partner. Find out what your partner thinks about his or her health. Use the questions below and your own questions. Get more information if necessary.

- Do you like to exercise?
- Do you think you are healthy?
- Do you like to eat a snack between meals? Do you think it's healthy?
- Do you read or watch TV shows about health or exercise?

Example:

A: Do you think you are healthy?

B: Yes.

A: Please explain.

B: Well, I exercise every day, and I always eat healthy food.

6 Tell the class about your partner.

Example:

Kim likes to exercise. She goes to a health club every day. She swims on Mondays and Thursdays, and plays basketball every Saturday morning.

Read About It

 1 **Before You Read** Look at the picture. Where are the people? What are they doing? Read the title of the reading. What do you think *working out* means? What do you think the reading is about?

Working Out at Work

A lot of people are out of shape. They say that they don't have time to exercise or to eat right. For this reason, many companies are now providing exercise centers and health classes for their workers.

Workers in both large and small companies can exercise during their lunch hour. For example, at Texas Instruments, Inc., in Dallas, there is an exercise center with fitness instructors and nutrition classes for the 22,000 employees. At one of Nike's locations, there is a weight machine, two exercise bicycles, and two rowing machines for the 300 employees. British Rail at Waterloo Station in London also has an exercise room for its employees.

At Bonnie Bell in Ohio, employees get thirty more minutes at lunch time if they want to exercise, and they can wear exercise clothes at work in the afternoon. If a Bonnie Bell employee exercises four days a week for half a year, he or she gets $250 from the company!

It is important to be healthy and in shape. But don't wait for your company or school to start a health program. You can eat right and start your own exercise routine right now.

company:	place to work
provide:	have
fitness:	health
nutrition:	healthy eating
employee:	worker
half:	$\frac{1}{2}$

rowing machine

2 Read the article. Then check (✓) **T** for True and **F** for False or **Don't know**. Explain your answers.

		T	F	Don't know
a.	Workers at many companies can exercise at work.	☐	☐	☐
b.	Small companies don't have health programs for their workers.	☐	☐	☐
c.	At Texas Instruments, Inc., 22,000 people exercise every day.	☐	☐	☐
d.	Workers can go to classes on healthy eating at Texas Instruments, Inc.	☐	☐	☐
e.	Bonnie Bell employees can get money if they exercise a lot.	☐	☐	☐
f.	A lot of people at Bonnie Bell wear exercise clothes at work.	☐	☐	☐
g.	Don't start your own exercise routine. Wait for your company or school to start a health program.	☐	☐	☐

3 Work with a partner. Discuss the questions. Then tell the class what you think.

a. Do you think health programs for students and workers are good? Explain.

b. Can you be healthy and not exercise? Explain.

c. Can you exercise but not be healthy? Explain.

d. Does your school or company have an exercise program? Can it start one?

Write About It

 4 **Before You Write** What does a good health club have? Share your ideas with your partner.

5 **Write** You and your partner work at a health club. You want new members. Write an advertisement about your club. Use the ad on page 66 as a model. Name your health club. Draw pictures of activities at your club. Write about what you can do there. Tell the address and the hours the club is open.

 6 **Check Your Writing** Work with another pair of students. Read each other's ads. Correct your sentences. Write the final copy.

> • Are the verbs correct?
> • Are the adverbs of frequency correct?
> • Is the spelling correct?

GETTING STARTED

Warm Up

1 Match each picture with the correct word.

1. _____	6. _____
2. _____	7. _____
3. _____	8. _____
4. _____	9. _____
5. _____	

angry	worried	shocked
sad	nervous	tired
sick	happy	afraid

2 Look at the pictures. Work with a partner. Ask and answer questions about feelings.

Example:

A: What is the girl in picture 7 doing?

B: She's sitting in bed.

A: How does she feel?

B: She feels sick.

Can't we be friends?

3 Listen and read.

In the last *Soap Suds* magazine, David and Mona were in love. But today something happened …

4 Answer the questions.

a. Does David love Mona?

b. Did Mona love David yesterday?

c. Does Mona love David now?

d. Who does Mona love?

e. Why is David confused?

f. Do you think Mona and David can be friends? Explain.

Building Vocabulary

Feelings

 5 Work with a partner. Ask and answer questions about how you feel. Use these words. You can answer with more than one word.

afraid	sick	healthy
confused	thirsty	nervous
happy	worried	sad
hungry	angry	tired
shocked	great	

a. You win $1,000. How do you feel?

b. You have an important English test now. How do you feel?

c. You lifted weights for fifty minutes. How do you feel?

d. You're in a plane for the first time. How do you feel?

e. You want to eat. How do you feel?

f. Your family buys a new car. How do you feel?

g. Your grandmother is sick. How do you feel?

h. Your good friend is crying. How do you feel?

i. A strange man is following you. How do you feel?

Adverbs of Time

Then	Now	Then	Now
yesterday	today	last week	this week
yesterday morning	this morning	last month	this month
yesterday afternoon	this afternoon	last year	this year
last night	tonight/this evening	last Thursday	this Monday

6 Work with a partner. Where were you? Where was your partner? Ask and answer questions. Complete the chart.

Example:

A: Where were you yesterday afternoon?

B: I was at the health club. Where were you?

A: I was at the mall.

Where were you … ?	I …	My partner …
a. yesterday afternoon?		
b. last night?		
c. last Sunday?		
d. last month?		
e. last year?		

Talk About It

7 Look at the chart in Exercise 6. Tell the class where you and your partner were.

Example:

I was at the mall yesterday afternoon. Ofra was at the health club.

GRAMMAR

The Simple Past Tense with *Be*: Statements and Yes/No Questions

To talk about the past, we use the simple past tense. The simple past tense of the verb *be* is *was* (singular) and *were* (plural).

Statements	Yes/No Questions	Short Answers
I **was** tired yesterday.	**Were** you tired?	Yes, I **was**./No, I **wasn't**.
You **were** worried about Sam.	**Were** you nervous?	Yes, I **was**./No, I **wasn't**.
She **was** sad yesterday.	**Was** she sick?	Yes, she **was**./No, she **wasn't**.
They **were** in Peru last week.	**Were** they happy?	Yes, they **were**./No, they **weren't**.

note **Contractions:** was not = wasn't
were not = weren't

1 Complete the story with words from the box.

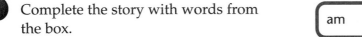
| am | is | are | was | were |

Last week, Mona **(1.)** _____
David's girlfriend. Last week, Mona and David **(2.)** _____
in love. Today, Mona **(3.)** _____ not in love with David.
She **(4.)** _____ in love with another man. Mona says,
"You **(5.)** _____ my good friend."

David **(6.)** _____ not happy. David says, "I **(7.)** _____
shocked and confused. How can we be friends?" Mona says,
"I **(8.)** _____ your girlfriend for
eight months. I **(9.)** _____ sorry,
but it's time to stop. Here **(10.)** _____
your ring. I want to return it. There
(11.) _____ another girl for you,
David." David says, "Ohhh! Last week
you **(12.)** _____ my love, and
now you want to be my friend. Good-bye,
Mona. I need to be alone!"

The Simple Past Tense: Information Questions with *Be*

To ask information questions with *be* in the past, we use a question word and *was* or *were*.

Information Questions	Answers
Who was angry?	Sally's boyfriend **was** angry.
Why was he angry?	He **was** angry because Sally **wasn't** with him last night.
How long was he angry?	He **was** angry for two hours.
Where were you yesterday?	We **were** at the mall.
When were you there?	We **were** there at eight o'clock.

2 Write the correct question for each answer.

a. (Where?) _____

Edgar was at the mall last night.

b. (When?) _____

He was there at 7:30.

c. (Who?) _____

He was with his wife.

d. (How long?) _____

They were at the mall for three hours.

e. (Where?) _____

They were in Style City.

f. (Why?) _____

They were in Style City because they returned a shirt.

g. (Who?) _____

The shirt was from his mother.

The Simple Past Tense: Regular Verbs

To form the simple past tense of regular verbs, we add *–ed* or *–d* to the verb. For negative statements, we use *did not + verb*.

Affirmative Statements	Negative Statements
I **played** basketball yesterday	He **didn't play** basketball yesterday.
You **watched** TV last night.	I **didn't watch** TV last night.
She **cooked** dinner last Thursday.	He **didn't cook** dinner last Thursday.
They **worked** every afternoon.	We **didn't work** every afternoon.

note cry = cried
stop = stopped

note **Contraction:** did not = didn't

The Simple Past Tense: Yes/No Questions and Short Answers

To ask yes/no questions about the past, we use *did* + verb.

Yes/No Questions	Short Answers
Did you **play** basketball on Sunday?	Yes, I **did**./No, I **didn't**.
Did he **work** last night?	Yes, he **did**./No, he **didn't**.
Did they **cook** dinner yesterday?	Yes, they **did**./No, they **didn't**.

3 Work with a partner. Ask and answer questions. Use the words in the box.

listen to	study	cook	talk
work out	exercise	dance	play
watch	walk	call	read

Example:

A: Did you talk to your mother yesterday?

B: Yes, I did.

A: Did you walk in the park yesterday?

B: No, I didn't. I worked out at the health club.

The Simple Past Tense: Information Questions

To ask information questions in the past, we use a question word and *did* + verb.

Questions	Answers
What did you **do** yesterday?	I **watched** a soap opera.
Where did you **watch** it?	I **watched** it at my house.
Who did you **watch** it with?	I **watched** it with my mother.
How long did you **watch** it?	We **watched** it for one hour.
When did you **call** Melissa?	I **called** Melissa at eight o'clock.
Why did you **call** her?	I **called** her because I needed to talk to her.

4 Work with a partner. Ask and answer questions.

When		watch on TV last week?
Where		play basketball?
Who	did you	want to study English?
Why		smile at today?
What		exercise at the health club?
How long		live last year?

Object Pronouns

We use object pronouns after verbs and prepositions.

Subject	Object	
I	me	He loves **me**.
he	him	
she	her	
it	it	I like **it**.
we	us	
you	you	
they	them	We aren't angry with **them**.

5 Complete the story with the correct pronoun.

My husband loves the theater. I go with **(1.)** _____ every
Friday night. Our daughter and son go with **(2.)** _____. I talk
in the theater a lot. My family gets angry with **(3.)** _____
and says, "Be quiet! We're listening to the actors, not to **(4.)** _____."
But I'm not angry with **(5.)** _____ because they're my family.

Then we go to our favorite place to eat, Pasta Pronto. We like
(6.) _____ a lot. The people there know **(7.)** _____
and say hello. They like our daughter a lot, and they always smile
at **(8.)** _____.

6 **Express Yourself** Find someone who did each activity in the chart.
Ask your classmates. Write the classmate's name in the correct box.
Then tell the class about five classmates.

Examples:

ALAN: Did you walk in the park last Sunday?
TOM: No, I didn't.
ALAN: What did you do?
TOM: I exercised at the health club.

watched TV last night	listened to music this morning	walked in the park last Sunday
returned a video to the store yesterday	called a friend last night	waited for a bus this week
didn't go to the movies last Saturday	worked on a computer	exercised at the health club last weekend

LISTENING and SPEAKING

Listen: *The World Is Small*—A Radio Soap Opera

STRATEGY ▶ **1** **Before You Listen** Look at the people in the picture. Where are they? What are they doing? How do you think they feel? What do you think they are talking about?

🎧 **2** Read the questions. Listen to the soap opera. Circle the best answer.

1. What is wrong with Maria?
   a. Maria thinks Roberto loves another woman.
   b. Maria thinks Antonio doesn't love her.
   c. Maria thinks she doesn't love Antonio or Roberto.

2. Why didn't Maria talk to Roberto in the park?
   a. Antonio was with her.
   b. She was angry and confused.
   c. She didn't like him.

3. How does Maria feel?
   a. She feels afraid and confused.
   b. She feels alone, but happy.
   c. She feels confused and alone.

Pronunciation

🎧 **3** Listen and read.

The –ed Ending

In English, we pronounce the –ed ending three ways:

/t/	/d/	/ɪd/
stopp**ed**	play**ed**	need**ed**

🎧 **4** Listen to each verb. Check the –ed sound you hear.

		/t/	/d/	/ɪd/			/t/	/d/	/ɪd/
a.	returned	☐	☐	☐	d.	watched	☐	☐	☐
b.	wanted	☐	☐	☐	e.	cooked	☐	☐	☐
c.	called	☐	☐	☐	f.	waited	☐	☐	☐

Speak Out

STRATEGY ▶ **Expressing Shock** To show you feel shocked about something, you can say:

What? That can't be true.	I can't believe it!
What are you saying?	I'm shocked.
---

5 Work with a partner or in small groups. Look at the conversation between David and Mona on page 76.

   a. Write a new conversation between David and Mona, or between Mona and her new boyfriend, or between David and his new girlfriend. Show that one person is shocked about something.

      Example:

      DAVID: Mona, I'd like you to meet my new girlfriend. Linda, this is Mona.

      LINDA: Hi, Mona. Nice to meet you.

      MONA: David. What are you saying? Your new girlfriend? That can't be true!

   b. Practice your conversation with your partner. Then act it out for the class.

READING and WRITING

Read About It

STRATEGY **1** **Before You Read** Look quickly at the reading. What soap opera is the reading about? What people are in it? What days is it on?

What Happened in the Soaps Last Week?

Susan   Frank   Billy

Family Trees

Monday
Susan didn't work for ten years. Then she wanted to start teaching again. But she thought that Frank, her husband, didn't want her to work. Susan was very sad and confused. She didn't know what to do. Susan called her friend Angela. She talked to her about her problem. Angela said, "Follow your heart. You love to teach. Talk to Frank."

again:	another time
said:	past tense of *say*

Billy, Susan's son, asked a new girlfriend to go to the mall with him.

Tuesday
Billy is having problems in school. Billy's teacher called Susan and said that he didn't study, listen, or do his homework. Susan cried. She was very worried. Susan talked to Billy about school, but he didn't want to talk about it. All he wanted to do was be with his new girlfriend.

Susan waited for Frank to come home. She wanted to talk to him about their son. Frank didn't come home until ten o'clock. Susan was in bed. She didn't talk to him about anything.

Wednesday
Susan talked to Frank in the morning. He called Billy's teacher. At work, Frank talked to some men about their wives. A lot of their wives worked. He was confused. Their family needed money, but he wanted Susan to be at home for Billy.

Susan looked in the newspaper for a job. Billy went to the mall again with his new girlfriend. He didn't study for his test.

Read the article. Circle **T** for True or **F** for False. Explain your answers.

a. Susan was a teacher.   **T**   **F**

b. Billy asked Angela to go to the mall.   **T**   **F**

c. Susan is worried about her son.   **T**   **F**

d. Frank doesn't want Susan to work.   **T**   **F**

e. Susan talked to Frank about Billy on Tuesday night.   **T**   **F**

f. Billy and his new girlfriend were at the mall Wednesday.   **T**   **F**

g. Frank talked to some people about their wives at work.   **T**   **F**

h. Susan's family needs money.   **T**   **F**

Write About It

STRATEGY 3 **Before You Write** Look at the pictures of Susan and her family. What happened in *Family Trees* on Thursday and Friday?

Thursday

Friday

 4 **Write** Write a paragraph about the soap opera. Use the pictures. Use the simple past tense to tell what happened.

5 **Check Your Writing** Work with a partner. Read each other's paragraphs. Correct your sentences. Write the final copy.

- Does the paragraph tell what happened?
- Are the past tense verbs correct?
- Are the adverbs of time correct?
- Is the spelling correct?

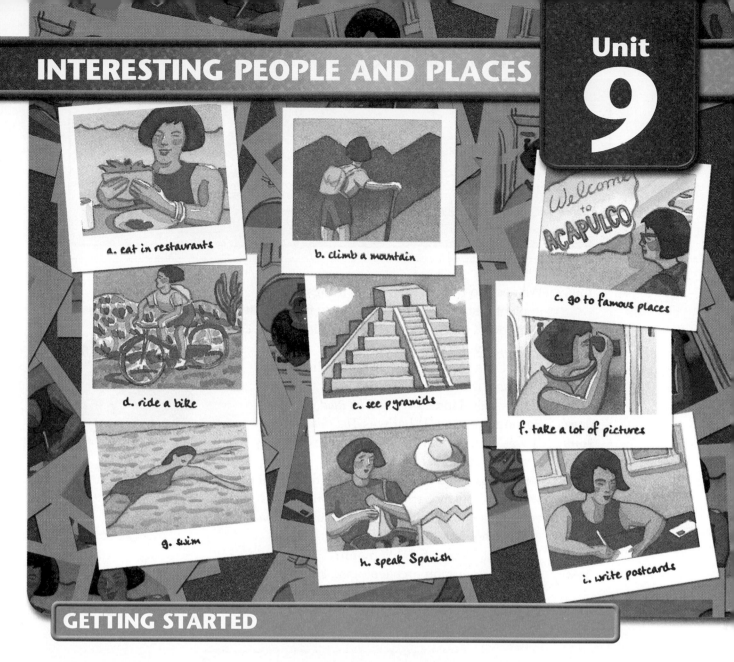

a. eat in restaurants

b. climb a mountain

c. go to famous places

d. ride a bike

e. see pyramids

f. take a lot of pictures

g. swim

h. speak Spanish

i. write postcards

Welcome to ACAPULCO

GETTING STARTED

Warm Up

1 Miriam is going on vacation. Look at the pictures. What does she want to do?

2 Miriam got back from her vacation in Mexico yesterday. What did she do? Work with a partner. Tell what Miriam did.

Example:

A: Where did Miriam eat?

B: She ate in some good restaurants.

a. ate	**b.** climbed	**c.** went
d. rode	**e.** saw	**f.** took
g. swam	**h.** spoke	**i.** wrote

Did you study for the test yet?

🎧 **3** Listen and read.

A. **JOHN:** We need to remember a lot of things for our ancient history test. Did you study for the test? Why don't you ask me some questions first. Then I can ask you some questions.

MARK: Fine. Let's see … first question. Who wrote *The Iliad*?

JOHN: That's easy. Homer wrote *The Iliad*.

MARK: Second question. What was *The Iliad* about?

JOHN: It was about a war between Greece and Troy.

MARK: Was it about a real war?

JOHN: Yes, it was. For a long time, people thought the war didn't really happen. They thought *The Iliad* was just a story. But Heinrich Schliemann read it, and he thought it was true.

MARK: Who was Heinrich Schliemann?

JOHN: He was a German archaeologist. He looked for the ruins of Troy and found them in the 1870s.

MARK: Did the Trojans win the war?

JOHN: No. They lost.

ancient: very old

Troy

Trojans: people from Troy

Stonehenge

B. **JOHN:** OK. Now I want to ask some questions. Who built Stonehenge and when?

MARK: Ancient people in England built it in about 1800 B.C. We don't really know who they were or how they did it, but we know what they did there.

JOHN: What did they do at Stonehenge?

MARK: They watched and studied the sun, the moon, and the stars, and they made a calendar.

C.

JOHN: All right. Here are the last questions. Where are the ruins of the famous Mayan city of Tikal?

MARK: Oh, that's easy. They're in Guatemala.

JOHN: When did the Mayas live there?

MARK: They started to build stone buildings there in about 900 B.C. They lived there to about A.D. 900.

JOHN: That's right! OK. I think we learned a lot. We're ready for our test now.

Tikal

4 These questions were on John and Mark's history test. Circle the correct answers.

1. What was *The Iliad* about?
   a. a real war
   b. a war that never happened
   c. Heinrich Schliemann's discoveries

2. Who won the Trojan War?
   a. the Trojans
   b. the Greeks
   c. No one. It never happened.

3. Who discovered the ruins of Troy?
   a. Homer
   b. the ancient Greeks
   c. Heinrich Schliemann

4. Where is Stonehenge?
   a. Greece
   b. England
   c. Guatemala

5. Where is Tikal?
   a. Greece
   b. England
   c. Guatemala

6. Who built Tikal?
   a. the Greeks
   b. the Trojans
   c. the Mayas

Building Vocabulary

 5 **Vocabulary Check** Write the letter of the correct picture on the line.

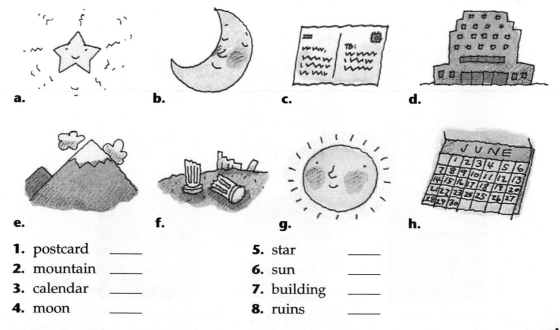

a.   **b.**   **c.**   **d.**

e.   **f.**   **g.**   **h.**

1. postcard _____
2. mountain _____
3. calendar _____
4. moon _____

5. star _____
6. sun _____
7. building _____
8. ruins _____

Ordinal Numbers

Cardinal numbers tell how many.
Ordinal numbers tell the order.

> Joe's building has thirteen (13) floors.
>
> Joe lives on the **thirteenth** (13th) floor.
>
> We had two (2) tests yesterday.
>
> The **second** (2nd) test was easy.

thirteenth (13th)
twelfth (12th)
eleventh (11th)
tenth (10th)
ninth (9th)
eighth (8th)
seventh (7th)
sixth (6th)
fifth (5th)
fourth (4th)
third (3rd)
second (2nd)
first (1st)

Dates

In speaking, we use ordinal numbers with dates.

> Her birthday is **March 23rd** (March twenty-third).
>
> I was born on **September 14th** (September fourteenth), **1981.***
>
> * We <u>write</u> September 14, 1981. We <u>say</u> September 14th, 1981

note We pronounce years in different ways.

1800 = eighteen hundred
1904 = nineteen-oh-four
1917 = nineteen seventeen

1979 = nineteen seventy-nine
2000 = two thousand
2002 = two thousand two

6 When do you think these famous people were born? Work with a partner. Compare your answers.

a. July 24, 1783   **c.** July 6, 1907   **e.** July 12, 100 B.C.
b. July 24, 1898   **d.** March 12, 1879   **f.** November 19, 1917

Example:

A: When do you think Albert Einstein was born?

B: I think he was born on March 12th, 1879.

1. Albert Einstein

2. Indira Gandhi

3. Simón Bolívar

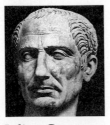

4. Julius Caesar

5. Frida Kahlo

6. Amelia Earhart

Talk About It

 Work in groups of three. Look at the chart. Ask and answer questions about when you did these things. Who was first? second? third? Then complete the chart. Write the names and the years.

	First	Second	Third
was born			
learned to ride a bike	*Sylvia: 1986*	*Juan: 1987*	*Ivan: 1989*
learned to swim			
took first airplane ride			
first spoke English			

Example:

IVAN:	When did you learn to ride a bike?
JUAN:	I learned to ride a bike in 1987. And you?
IVAN:	I learned in 1989. How about you, Sylvia?
SYLVIA:	I think it was in 1986.
IVAN:	OK, Sylvia, you were first!

GRAMMAR

The Simple Past Tense: Irregular Verbs

Many English verbs are irregular. These verbs do not end in –ed in the simple past tense.

	Past		Past		Past
buy	**bought**	go	**went**	speak	**spoke**
build	**built**	have	**had**	swim	**swam**
come	**came**	lose	**lost**	take	**took**
do	**did**	make	**made**	think	**thought**
eat	**ate**	read	**read**	win	**won**
find	**found**	ride	**rode**	write	**wrote**
get	**got**	see	**saw**		

Questions	Answers
Where **did** Carol **lose** her ring?	She **lost** it at the health club.
Did she **find** it?	Yes, she **did**. (No she **didn't**.)
	She **found** it in the weight room.
When **did** she **buy** the ring?	She **bought** it last week.

1 Complete the sentences with the simple past tense of the verbs.

   a. Homer (write) _____ a book about a war between Troy and Greece.

   b. Heinrich Schliemann (think) _____ *The Iliad* was true.

   c. Schliemann (find) _____ the ruins of Troy in the 1870s.

   d. The Greeks (win) _____ the war, and the Trojans (lose) _____.

   e. Ancient people (build) _____ Stonehenge in about 1800 B.C.

   f. The people (make) _____ a calendar at Stonehenge.

2 Write information questions for the underlined words.

   a. _____?

      <u>Last month</u> Miriam took a vacation in Mexico.

   b. _____?

      She was there for <u>two weeks</u>.

   c. _____?

      She read <u>a book about Mexico City</u>.

   d. _____?

      She rode a bus to <u>the ancient city of Tenochtitlán</u>.

   e. _____?

      Miriam spoke Spanish on her trip <u>because she studied it in school</u>.

3 Work with a partner. One partner looks at Time Line A. The other looks at Time Line B on page 94. Ask questions to find out the information you don't have.

   Example:

   A: Who built the city of Tikal?   **A:** When did the Mayas build the city?

   B: The Mayas built the city of Tikal.   **B:** They built it in 900 B.C.

Time Line A		
	The _____ built the city of Tikal in Guatemala.	
	The Greeks played in the first Olympic Games.	
	Heinrich Schliemann found _____.	
1911	Hiram Bingham found the city of Machu Picchu.	
1969	Neil Armstrong walked on the moon.	
	Scientists in _____ built the first World Wide Web.	

 4 **Express Yourself** What did you do last week? Check (✓) *yes* or *no* in the chart on page 91. What did your partner do? Check (✓) *yes* or *no*. Ask and answer questions.

   Example:

   A: Did you buy any new books last week?

   B: No, I didn't. Did you?

   A: Yes, I did. I bought a book about the Mayas.

	You		Your Partner	
	Yes	No	Yes	No
buy some new books	☐	☐	☐	☐
take a test	☐	☐	☐	☐
take some pictures	☐	☐	☐	☐
go to a friend's house	☐	☐	☐	☐
use a computer for homework	☐	☐	☐	☐
speak English with a friend	☐	☐	☐	☐
see a video	☐	☐	☐	☐
write a letter	☐	☐	☐	☐
use the Internet	☐	☐	☐	☐

LISTENING and SPEAKING

Listen: People of the Past

 1 **Before You Listen** Look at the map. What do you know about these places?

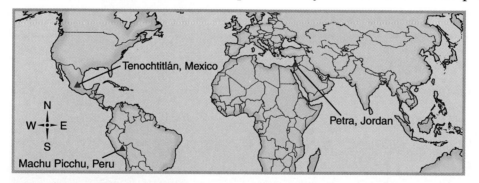

Tenochtitlán, Mexico

Petra, Jordan

Machu Picchu, Peru

N
W ⊕ E
S

2 Listen to the conversation. What did the students learn about these ancient people? Listen again to complete the chart. Check (✓) the boxes.

	Nabateans	Incas	Aztecs
a. had houses with one room			
b. had houses of red stone			
c. had buildings of white stone			
d. wrote with pictures			
e. lived in the mountains			

3 Listen to the conversation again. Correct your answers if necessary.

Pronunciation

🎧 **4** Listen and repeat.

/θ/		
think	bir**th**day	mon**th**
third	heal**th**y	tru**th**

🎧 **5** Listen to the words. Check (✓) *yes* when you hear the sound /θ/ in think. Check *no* when you don't.

	Yes	No			Yes	No			Yes	No			Yes	No
a.	☐	☐		**c.**	☐	☐		**e.**	☐	☐		**g.**	☐	☐
b.	☐	☐		**d.**	☐	☐		**f.**	☐	☐		**h.**	☐	☐

Speak Out

STRATEGY ▶ **Using Time Expressions** We use time expressions to talk about the order of events.

> **PAULA:** Yesterday my family and I went to Yosemite National Park. We had a great time. **First**, we climbed a mountain. **Then** we rode our bikes. **After that**, we ate lunch.
>
> **WANDA:** Did you see any bears?

6 Think about a family vacation.

- Where did you go?
- How long were you there?
- What did you see?
- What did you eat?
- What did you do?
- What did you buy?
- When did you go?
- Who went with you?

Work in a small group and talk about a place you went with your family. Use time expressions to show the order of events.

READING and WRITING

Read About It

STRATEGY **1** **Before You Read** First, look at the photo and the title of the reading. Then look at the word map. What do you think the reading is about?

```
┌────────────────────┐                    ┌──────────────────────────────┐
│ was born           │                    │ discovered _____ .  │
│ in _____ .   │                    └──────────────────────────────┘
└────────────────────┘         ┌──────────────────┐
                               │  Hiram Bingham   │
┌────────────────────┐         └──────────────────┘
│ was a              │                    ┌──────────────────────────────┐
│ _____ teacher.│                   │ died in _____ .     │
└────────────────────┘                    └──────────────────────────────┘
```

2 Complete the word map in Exercise 1.

Hiram Bingham and the Lost City of Machu Picchu

Hiram Bingham (1875–1956) was a history teacher. He wanted to learn about the ancient people of South America. He visited South America five 5 times and discovered many ancient ruins. His most famous discovery was in Peru. It was the ruins of Machu Picchu, the lost city of the Incas.

The Incas lived in South America 10 for 300 years. Then, in the 1500s, they lost a war with the Spanish. The Spanish tried to destroy everything that the Incas built, but people said there was still an old city somewhere in 15 the mountains.

Machu Picchu

destroy: make into ruins
still: at that time
told time: learned what time

Many people searched for Machu Picchu, but no one found it. Then, in 1911, Bingham learned about some ruins on a mountain, next to the Urubamba River. Bingham climbed the mountain, and there was the city!

At one time, 1,000 people lived in Machu Picchu. They built long streets and 20 beautiful stone buildings. One building was an observatory where they watched the sun, moon, and stars. They told time by the stars and made a calendar to mark the hours, days, and years.

When did these people leave Machu Picchu? Where did they go? No one knows.

Today tourists can take buses up to these famous ruins. They walk on the streets 25 and take pictures of the houses. They like to go to this ancient place.

3 Read the article. Find each word in the reading. Circle the answer that means the same.

1. **visited** (line 4)   **a.** read about   **b.** looked for   **c.** went to

2. **lost** (line 8)   **a.** not won   **b.** not found   **c.** old

3. **searched for** (line 16) **a.** talked about it   **b.** saw   **c.** looked for

4. **tourists** (line 24)   **a.** people on   **b.** people on   **c.** bus drivers
                                  business   vacation

5. **up** (line 24)   **a.** ↓   **b.** ↑   **c.** ←

Write About It

4 **Before You Write** Look at Maria's time line.

1981	1984	1986	1988	1993	1996	1999
born in Juarez, Mexico	moved to Mexico City	studied piano	first day of school	visited San Antonio, Texas	moved to Los Angeles, California	started college

Make a time line of your life on a piece of paper.

5 **Write** Write five sentences about your life. Use information from the time line.

6 **Check Your Writing** Work with a partner. Read your partner's time line and sentences. Correct your sentences. Write the final copy.

- Are the regular past tense verbs correct?
- Are the irregular past tense verbs correct?
- Is the spelling correct?

Time Line B	
900 B.C.	The Mayas built the city of Tikal in Guatemala.
776 B.C.	The Greeks played in the first Olympic Games.
1870	Heinrich Schliemann found the ruins of Troy.
	_____ found the city of Machu Picchu.
	Neil Armstrong _____.
1989	Scientists in Switzerland built the first World Wide Web.

1 Complete the paragraph with the correct form of the verbs. Use the simple present or the present progressive tense.

Lucinda **(1. work)** _____ for a newspaper in San Francisco. She **(2. want)** _____ to write about Mexican cooking, but she **(3. know,** *neg.***)** _____ how to cook Mexican food. Lucinda's grandmother **(4. be)** _____ a great cook! That is why Lucinda **(5. take)** _____ her vacation at her grandmother's house in Texas this week. Lucinda **(6. learn)** _____ how to cook. She **(7. watch)** _____ her grandmother, and she **(8. write)** _____ down her grandmother's ideas about good food. Lucinda **(9. love)** _____ her grandmother's Mexican cooking a lot, but she is afraid she **(10. get)** _____ out of shape.

2 Complete the conversations with *me, him, her, it, us,* or *them.*

1. ROBERT: Look, Albert. There's an apple pie on the table.
   ALBERT: Ummm. Let's eat _____ now.

2. SAM: I think Mrs. Gonzalez is our salesperson.
   RONA: Let's ask _____ about short sleeve shirts.

3. ALICE: The people at this party are nice.
   JULIO: Let's talk to some of _____.

4. JIM: Did your boyfriend call you last night?
   KIM: No. I called _____.

5. SUMI: Are you going to the movies tonight?
   LAURA: Yes. Do you want to come with _____?

6. WENDY: Hi, Jamie. What are you doing?
   JAMIE: My father and I are going to join the health club. Do you want to come with _____?

3 Write the information question for each answer. Use the simple past tense.

1. _____
Alice went <u>to Australia</u> on vacation.

2. _____
She went there <u>because she wanted to see</u> the Outback.

3. _____
She went with <u>her friend Jeanne</u>.

4. _____
They were there <u>for two weeks</u>.

5. _____
They climbed <u>Uluru (Ayer's Rock)</u>.

6. _____
Alice wrote a lot of postcards to <u>her boyfriend</u>.

7. _____

She wrote to him <u>every day</u>!

8. _____

They got home <u>last week</u>.

4 Make sentences. Match the words in Column A with the words in Column B.

	Column A		Column B
1. ____	Olivia watches	**a.**	at the mall today.
2. ____	Melissa needs	**b.**	to exercise.
3. ____	Gary is watching	**c.**	on vacation last week.
4. ____	Patrick lost	**d.**	a video now.
5. ____	Please meet me	**e.**	two soap operas on TV every day.
6. ____	Don't eat	**f.**	a letter to her friend.
7. ____	Teddy went	**g.**	those green tomatoes.
8. ____	Don't follow	**h.**	his ring at the health club.
9. ____	Today Miriam wrote	**i.**	me. I want to be alone.

Vocabulary Review

Complete the conversations with words from the box.

confused	favorite
calendar	month
member	remember
discover	snacks
exercise	worried
healthy	climb
third	

A. **LAURA:** Do you **(1.)** _____ the date of Shirley's birthday?

  BILL: No, I don't, but I can look on my **(2.)** _____.

  LAURA: I think it's this **(3.)** _____.

B. **ALLEN:** Are you a **(4.)** _____ of Gold's Gym?

  BARBARA: Yes, I am. I try to keep in shape. I **(5.)** _____ every day!

  ALLEN: Do you eat **(6.)** _____ foods?

  BARBARA: Yes, and I eat a lot of **(7.)** _____, too.

  ALLEN: Oh, what's your **(8.)** _____ snack?

  BARBARA: Pizza.

C. **ERIN:** I'm **(9.)** _____ about the Spanish test this week.

  GINA: Me, too. The grammar is hard. I'm **(10.)** _____.

  ERIN: Let's study at the library tonight.

D. **CINDY:** Weren't you on vacation last week? Didn't you **(11.)** _____ some famous mountain?

  FLORA: Yes. It was my **(12.)** _____ climb up that mountain.

  CINDY: Did you **(13.)** _____ anything new?

  FLORA: Yes, I'm getting old.

SERVICES

a. GET READY FOR A GOOD JOB! Study at Cyber Technical School. We can teach you to use a computer in one week! Classes in word processing start every week. Internet classes, too. Don't wait! Call for more information any day before 9 p.m. We're at 1946 Park Street. Our telephone number is (708) 555-0700; our fax number is (708) 555-0701.

b. IS YOUR HOUSE DIRTY? Do you need someone to clean it? Call House of Clean! Our people can clean anything and they can come anytime. Call us today at (815) 354-2441 and have a clean house tonight!

c. CHOMSKY'S LANGUAGE SCHOOL. Would you like to learn Portuguese? We can teach you to speak Portuguese, Spanish, French, Italian, German, Russian, Arabic, or Japanese. We have classes for adults and children. We have classes in the morning, afternoon, and evening, and on weekends. CALL TODAY, at (708) 375-7676, or come to our office at 675 Park Street.

d. DO YOU WANT TO GET IN SHAPE AND BE THIN? Come and work out here. Lose that fat! At LA Health Club, we have early morning classes and late evening classes. Come in for one free class! Address: 1410 Lake Avenue. Phone: (708) 375-0909

e. WE NEED YOU TO BE OUR REPORTERS AND WRITE NEWS ARTICLES FOR US! Tell us what's happening in the city. We're here every day, 24 hours a day. WNTC Radio. 1232 Lake Avenue. Come for an interview or call us at (708) 555-7575 with your news. You can also fax us at (708) 555-7576.

RETAIL SALES

f. ARE YOU TALL? DO YOU NEED TO WEAR BIG CLOTHES? Come to Highland Big and Tall Men's Store. 25% off sale on all pants this weekend! 250 Mountain View Road, in the Mountain Town Mall. (815) 354-6057.

g. ONE DAY ONLY SALE! All baby clothes and toys. On sale today at Cooper's Children's Place, 927 Sierra St. We open early and close late: 7 a.m. to 10 p.m. Phone: (708) 375-8976.

GETTING STARTED

Warm Up

 Work with a partner. Look at the ads. Match each question with the correct ad.

1. _____ Your father is very tall. You want to buy him some pants for his birthday. Where can you go?

2. _____ You'd like your son to learn Italian. Where can he go?

3. _____ Your house is dirty, but you don't have time to clean it. Who can you call?

4. _____ Your mother wants to buy some toys for your baby. Where can she go?

5. _____ You and your friends saw a famous actor at the health club. You think this is interesting news. Who can you call?

6. _____ You want to lose some weight. Where can you go?

2 Work with a partner. Ask and answer questions with *what, where, when,* and *who.*

Example:

A: What can I learn at Cyber Technical School?

B: To use a computer.

What do you think about it?

 3 Listen and read.

DOUG LEE: Good afternoon. I'm Doug Lee, a reporter for *TV News.* Welcome to *The People Speak.* Every week on this show I get opinions from people on the street about what's happening in the news. We have two stories today. Excuse me, ma'am. I'd like to ask you a question.

ANNA: All right. What is it?

DOUG LEE: First, can I ask your name please?

ANNA: Anna Romaro.

DOUG LEE: Thank you, Anna. Here's my question. The city wants to build a new mall with a tall office building next to the park. What do you think about it?

ANNA: Oh, I saw the design for that mall on TV. It's so big, and that office building is so tall and ugly. I don't want the city to build it next to the park. The neighborhood is pretty now.

DOUG LEE: Thank you for your opinion, Anna. What about you, sir? What's your name and what do you think?

BOB: I'm Bob Brown. I agree with her. I don't want them to build anything next to our pretty park. The city is making a big mistake.

DOUG LEE: And your name, miss? What's your opinion?

JULIA: My name is Julia Choi. Well, I disagree with them. I think the mall and the office building are a good idea. We need new businesses to come to our neighborhood. A lot of people like to shop and work in the same area.

DOUG LEE: Thank you very much for your opinion, Julia. Now for the second news report of the day. Excuse me, ma'am. Can I get your name please?

SONIA: Yes ... Sonia Hall.

DOUG LEE: I need your opinion, Sonia. City High School stopped all music classes. They said that they didn't have money. What do you think about that?

Sonia:	Oh, yes. I found out about that on the radio, and I was shocked and angry! I don't want the school to stop the music classes. My child loved them.	
Doug Lee:	And you, sir? What's your name and what do you think?	
Fernando:	Fernando Lopez. Well, Doug, ... I disagree with her. I think it's the right thing to do. The school needed to stop something. There's no money. And students don't need to learn music.	
Doug Lee:	Thank you very much. That's all the time we have. Do you have an opinion about something in the news? Call our hot line, at 708-555-7575, and tell us your opinion! For *The People Speak,* I'm Doug Lee.	

4 Answer the questions.

a. What does Doug Lee do?

b. Who is Doug Lee talking to today? Why?

c. Do you watch opinion shows on TV or listen to them on the radio? Do you like them? Why or why not?

5 Doug Lee wrote some notes about the people he interviewed. Complete the information.

News Story 1: The city wants to _____ next to the park.

Name: Opinion: Reason:

1. _Anna Romaro_____   _____   _____

2. _____   _He agrees with Anna._   _____

3. _____   _____   _____

News Story 2: City High School stopped _____

_____

Name: Opinion: Reason:

1. _____   _____   _____

2. _____   _____   _____

Building Vocabulary

 6 **Vocabulary Check** *Happy* and *sad* are opposites.
Write the opposite of each word.

a. small ___*large*___   e. early _____

b. short _____   f. agree _____

c. clean _____   g. ugly _____

d. thin _____   h. ask _____

Phone Numbers

These are North American telephone numbers. Say them like this:

555-8347

(219) 725-3363
area code two-one-nine, seven-two-five, three-three-six-three
555-0900
five-five-five, oh-nine hundred

Addresses

Say addresses like this:

250 Park Avenue = two-fifty Park Avenue
1456 Green Street = fourteen-fifty-six Green Street

7 Work with a partner. Ask and answer questions about the telephone numbers and addresses in the ads on page 97.

Example:

A: Where's Cyber Technical School?

B: The address is nineteen-forty-six Park Street.

A: And the phone number?

B: Area code seven-oh-eight, five-five-five, oh-seven hundred.

A: Thanks.

B: You're welcome.

Talk About It

8 Work with a partner. Ask and answer information questions about a place in your neighborhood.

Example:

A: Where can I get some chocolate ice cream?

B: At Luigi's ice-cream shop.

A: What's the address?

B: It's thirty-seven High Street.

A: Thanks!

9 Practice your conversation with your partner. Then act it out for the class.

GRAMMAR

Verb + Object + Infinitive

Some verbs are followed by an object + an infinitive.

want	I **want you to wait** for me.
ask	Please **ask your mother to call** me.
teach	Andrea **taught her sister to play** the piano.
need	Mr. Kocenda **needs you to answer** the phones today.
would like	I **would like you to stand** next to the door.
tell	Eva **told me not to wait** for her.

Questions	Answers
What do you **want me to do**?	I **want you to clean** your room.
When did you **ask her to call** you?	I **asked her to call** me last week.
Did Sylvia **teach Bill to swim**?	Yes, she did. She **taught him to swim** yesterday.
Do you **need me to go** to the store?	Yes, I **need you to buy** some milk.
Would you **like me to buy** those pants?	Yes, I**'d like you to buy** them.
What did he **tell you to do**?	He **told me not to cook** dinner.

Write sentences about yourself on a piece of paper. Use items from the box or ideas of your own.

Example:

My mother told me to do my homework.

My mother	want/wants		to clean (my) room.
My sister	asked		to close the door.
My brothers	tell/told	me	to write a letter for him/her.
My doctor	need/needs		to make dinner.
My friends	teach/taught		to be happy.
My teacher	would like		to do my homework.

 Work with a partner. Look at your partner's sentences. Did you have the same ideas?

 Look at the pictures. Work with a partner. Ask and answer questions.

Example:

A: What does she want him to do?

B: She wants him to close the window.

It's cold in here!

a.

You don't eat healthy food!

b.

Your room is dirty!

c.

I'm hungry!

d.

I need this in one hour!

e.

You didn't do your homework!

f.

4 **Express Yourself** Make two lists. In the first list, write three things someone taught you to do. In the second list, write three things you taught someone to do.

Example:

List 1	List 2
My mother taught me to use a computer.	*I taught my brother to ride a bike.*
My music teacher taught me to play the guitar.	*I taught my sister to jump rope.*
My father taught me to play basketball.	*I taught my friend to dance.*

Work with a partner. Take turns talking about your lists. Ask and answer questions.

Example:

A: My mother taught me to use a computer. Can you use a computer?

B: Yes, I can. My brother taught me to use a computer.

A: Did your brother teach you to ride a bike?

B: No, he didn't. My father taught me to ride a bike.

A: I taught my sister to play Nintendo.

B: Oh, my brother taught me. But, I taught my father to play Nintendo!

LISTENING and SPEAKING

Listen: What's Your Opinion?

 1 **Before You Listen** Where do you find out about the news? The newspaper? TV? radio? The Internet? Think about a story in the news this week. What's your opinion of the story?

2 Listen to the talk show *What's Your Opinion?* What are the people talking about? Circle the correct headlines.

City Streets Are Dirty

No Job Interviews on Weekdays

AFTER-SCHOOL SPORTS PROGRAM TO END

City to Build New Mall

No More City Money for Free Concerts

3 Listen again and complete the chart.

	City's Opinion	Gloria's Opinion	Peter's Opinion
First Problem			
Second Problem			

Pronunciation

 4 Listen and repeat.

/b/ and /v/			
berry **v**ery		**b**oat **v**ote	

5 Circle the words you hear.

a.	bat	vat	**e.**	bolt	volt
b.	bent	vent	**f.**	van	ban
c.	vile	bile	**g.**	bet	vet
d.	vest	best	**h.**	vane	bane

berry

Speak Out

STRATEGY **Agreeing and Disagreeing Politely** To agree or disagree politely with someone's opinion, you can say:

Agree	Disagree
I agree (with you).	I disagree (with you).
I think so, too.	I don't think so.
You're right.	I think you're wrong.
	I don't agree.

To show you aren't sure, you can say:

I'm not sure.	You could be right, but I think ...
I don't know about that.	Maybe ...

6 Work with a partner. Read the statements. Agree and disagree. Give your opinion and tell why you agree or disagree.

Example:

Tall office buildings and malls are a good idea for our neighborhood.

A: I agree with you because our community needs more people to work and live here.

B: I'm not sure I agree. We need buildings, but tall buildings are ugly. I like small buildings.

- **a.** Our class needs a new English textbook.
- **b.** Video games are good for children.
- **c.** There are a lot of good shows on TV.
- **d.** Students need to learn a second language in school.
- **e.** Parents need to read books to their sons and daughters.
- **f.** Every person needs to use a computer.
- **g.** Rock-and-roll music is terrible.
- **h.** Write your own _____.

READING and WRITING

Read About It

STRATEGY **1** **Before You Read** Look at the newspaper headlines.

a. **Famous Athlete Speaks at Library**

b. **City High School Students Study in Costa Rica**

c. **Women's Basketball Team Wins City Championship**

What do you want to know about each article?
Write a question for each headline.

2 Read each article. Match the headlines with the articles.

1. ____ Last Friday evening, former Chicago Bears star Michael Johnson spoke at the Hillsdale town library. Hundreds of children and adults, young and old, came to listen to the famous athlete talk about his life as a football player. The police closed the library doors at 7:30. They asked some people to stand outside, because there was no place to sit down inside the building.

Everyone stood up and cheered as Johnson walked into the library. He thanked the people and asked everyone to sit down. "I want to tell young people to work hard," Johnson said. "I want you to know that it is very hard work to be a great player, but you can do it." Johnson told young people in the audience four things. "First, you need to eat healthy food. Second, you need to work out every day. Third, you need to get lots of sleep. Last, you need to believe in yourself."

Johnson answered questions from the audience after he spoke. As he walked out of the building, he shook hands and gave autographs. Some people didn't agree with everything he said, but everyone enjoyed meeting him.

2. ____ East High School girl's basketball team won the city championship game last night. East High played West High in a very exciting game. The final score was 76–74.

More than 500 students and adults from both schools came to watch the two teams play in the East High School gym. "It was a great game," said East High coach, Helena Nagano. "East High won because we didn't get tired and we didn't make any mistakes," Nagano told reporters after the game. "I told the girls to play hard. They did, and we won."

Both teams played great basketball. In the last minute the score was tied at 74–74. Then Amanda Rivas of East High got the ball and ran down the court. She took a shot. It was good! East High won the game 76–74. The East High players were very happy, but the West High players were sad because they lost. "We're going to win next year," said West High coach Olga Tamirov.

3. _____ A group of students from City High School went to study in Costa Rica for six months. Five boys and four girls from the Spanish class traveled to San Jose in January. Each student lived with a different Costa Rican family.

The students went to La Paz Secondary School and studied math, science, history, and Spanish. They learned about Costa Rican history and customs. Usually the students spoke Spanish, but they met many people who wanted them to speak English, too.

When they left Costa Rica, they invited their new friends to visit the United States. Everyone agreed it was a great experience. The American and Costa Rican students promised to write to each other. One City High student said, "I would like everyone to have this kind of adventure."

3 News reporters answer four questions in every article. Look at the three articles you read in Exercise 2. Complete the following chart.

	Article 1	Article 2	Article 3
Who?			
What?			
Where?			
When?			

Write About It

4 **Before You Write** You are a reporter for your school newspaper. Get ready to write an article. Write about what happened in your class or in your school. Answer the four questions in your article.

Who? _____

What? _____

Where? _____

When? _____

5 **Write** Now write the article. Use the information from Exercise 4. Can you add other information? Can you answer the question _Why_, too?

6 **Check Your Writing** Work with a partner. Read each other's articles. Correct your articles. Write the final copy.

- Are all the _Wh–_ questions answered?
- Are the past tense verbs correct?
- Is the spelling correct?

Today's Horoscope Predictions for the Star Signs

Aquarius (January 20–February 18) A friend is going to introduce you to an important person who has the same star sign as you. Be ready!

Pisces (February 19–March 20) You are going to get news from another country.

Aries (March 21–April 19) You are going to disagree with a friend over a small problem.

Taurus (April 20–May 20) You are going to fall in love soon and get married. Follow your feelings!

Gemini (May 21–June 21) You are going to meet a famous scientist. Get ready to learn something new!

Cancer (June 22–July 22) You are going to discover something important.

Leo (July 23–August 22) A friend is going to need your help tomorrow.

Virgo (August 23–September 22) You are going to go on a vacation soon. Talk to a member of your family.

Libra (September 23–October 23) You are going to win a lot of money. Know who your friends are!

Scorpio (October 24–November 21) You are going to talk to an old friend. You will find out about something interesting from the past.

Sagittarius (November 22–December 21) You are going to hear some good news from an interesting person.

Capricorn (December 22–January 19) You are going to find something nice. Watch where you walk!

GETTING STARTED

Warm Up

1 Work with a partner. What is your partner's star sign? What does the horoscope predict about your partner?

Example:

A: When's your birthday?

B: June 29th.

A: You're a Cancer. It says you're going to discover something important.

B: How about you? When's your birthday?

A: October 11th.

B: Oh, you're a Libra. Let's see … It says you're going to win a lot of money.

A: Really? … That's amazing!

What does your horoscope say?

 2 Listen and read.

SUKI: Hi, Jenny. What are you doing?

JENNY: I'm reading my horoscope for today.

SUKI: Really? What's your sign? What does it say?

JENNY: Hmmm. I'm a Gemini. It says I'm going to meet a famous scientist.

SUKI: What about me?

JENNY: When were you born?

SUKI: September 19th. Look under Virgo.

JENNY: Let's see … Your horoscope is going to be different from mine. The stars predict that you are going to go on a vacation soon.

SUKI: That's amazing! Dan and I are going to visit our parents in Hawaii next weekend.

JENNY: Wow! That *is* amazing!

CHARLIE: Hi, Jenny! Hi, Suki! What's new?

JENNY: Charlie, listen. Suki's horoscope says she is going to go on a vacation soon, and it's true. She and Dan are going to visit their parents in Hawaii!

CHARLIE: You don't really believe in horoscopes, do you? They're not very scientific.

SUKI: What do you know? Are you some kind of scientist or something?

JENNY: Why, yes he is. Charlie is the school's "Scientist of the Year." You wrote a report about science in the future, didn't you, Charlie? You wrote all about new technologies. Didn't you say that computers are going to be able to help us do a lot of new things in the future?

CHARLIE: That's right, I did. Scientists can predict a lot of things about the future, too!

SUKI: There! You see, it's true! Jenny's horoscope prediction was right, too. She *did* meet a famous scientist today!

3 Answer the questions.

a. What does Suki's horoscope say? What is going to happen to her?

b. What is going to happen to Jenny?

c. Look at the horoscope predictions on page 107. What is Jenny's star sign?

d. Is Suki's horoscope true? Explain.

e. Is Jenny's horoscope true? Explain.

f. Who believes in horoscope readings? Who doesn't?

g. Why does Charlie know about the future?

Building Vocabulary

Weather

4 Look at the words in the list. Write the letter of the correct picture next to each word.

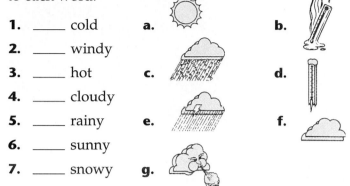

1. _____ cold   **a.**
2. _____ windy   **b.**
3. _____ hot   **c.**   **d.**
4. _____ cloudy
5. _____ rainy   **e.**   **f.**
6. _____ sunny
7. _____ snowy   **g.**

5 Look at the map of the United States. Predict the weather in different cities.

Example:

A: What's the weather going to be like in Los Angeles tomorrow?

B: It's going to be hot and sunny.

"Tomorrow's weather forecast is ..."

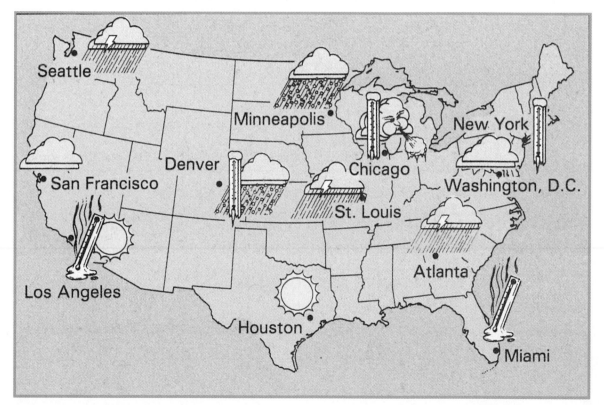

Prepositions of Direction

 6 Look at the picture. Write sentences about the picture on a piece of paper. Use *up*, *down*, *over*, *around*, and *under*.

Example:

A man is going down the building.

Talk About It

 7 Work in groups of eight. Look at the graph. How many people are going to do these things in the future?

Interview each person. For each *yes* answer, color a box on the graph. Compare your graphs. How are they the same? How are they different?

Example:

A: Are you going to buy a car in the future?

B: Yes, I am.

	buy a car	go to college	go around the world	get married	be famous	write a book	climb a mountain
8							
7							
6							
5							
4							
3							
2							
1							

GRAMMAR

The Future Tense with *Be going to*

We use *be going to* + verb to talk about the future.

Statements
I **am going to go** on vacation soon.
You **are going to win** a lot of money.
Jenny **is going to meet** a famous scientist.
They **are going to be** here at 6:00 p.m.
Suki and Dan **aren't going to visit** their parents this weekend.

1 Look at the graph for JoAnn's On-Line Bookstore. The graph shows:

how many books people bought this year

how many books people are going to buy next year

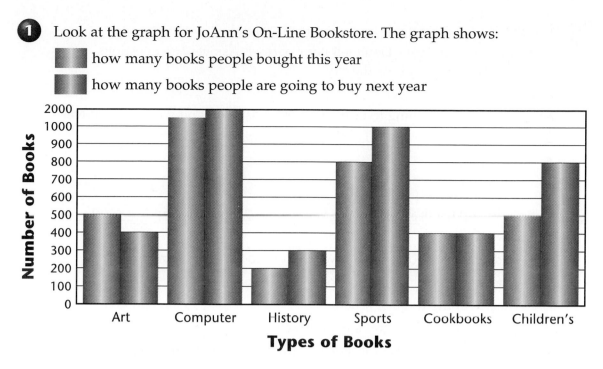

Types of Books

Use the graph to make predictions about next year. Answer the questions.

a. What types of books are people going to buy a lot of next year?
b. About how many history books are people going to buy next year?
c. What books are going to sell the same number this year?
d. How many books about sports are people going to buy?
e. What types of books are people not going to buy a lot of next year?

2 Look at the future times in the box. Make predictions about your life. What are you going to do at these times in the future? Write your answers on a piece of paper.

Example:

I'm going to go on vacation next year.

tomorrow	next year
in six months	next week
on Saturday	next month

The Future Tense with *Be going to*: Questions

Yes/No Questions	Short Answers
Is Joe **going to play** basketball tonight?	Yes, he is./No, he isn't./No, he's not.
Are you **going to get** a pizza for lunch?	Yes, we are./No, we aren't./No, we're not.

Wh– Questions	Answers
Where **is** Judy **going to go** tonight?	She **is going to go** to the movies.
What **is** she **going to see**?	She**'s going to see** *Star Wars 3*.
Who **is** she **going to go** with?	She**'s going to go** with her friends.

3 Work with a partner. Look at the weather map on page 109. Choose a city to visit tomorrow. Don't tell your partner. Ask yes/no questions about the weather to guess the city.

Example:

A: Is the weather going to be hot?   **A:** Are you going to go to Denver?

B: No, it isn't.   **B:** Yes, I am.

A: Is it going to be snowy?

B: Yes, it is.

 4 Work with a partner. Use the cues to ask *wh–* questions about the people.

Example:

Luis and Emma: school/tomorrow/eight o'clock in the morning

A: Where are Luis and Emma going to go tomorrow?

B: They're going to go to school.

A: What time are they going to go to school?

B: They're going to go to school at eight o'clock in the morning.

a. **Bruce:** the office/tomorrow/nine o'clock in the morning
b. **Magda:** the airport/Sunday/one o'clock
c. **Joe and Pedro:** the mall/tomorrow afternoon/four o'clock
d. **Anna and Karen:** the health club/this evening/seven o'clock
e. **Mark:** the language school/next Tuesday/9:40 a.m.
f. **Teddy:** the computer store/tomorrow morning/eleven o'clock

 5 Work with a partner. Read each sentence. What do you think these people are going to do? Ask and answer questions.

Example:

A: Susan has a new car.

B: Oh, really? What's she going to do?

A: She's going to drive to California. She's not going to take the bus.

a. Susan has a new car.	f. The Taylors are on vacation in Peru.
b. Tom just won $5,000.	g. Jason's clothes are dirty.
c. Frank loves Isabel.	h. Martha's birthday is next week.
d. John is sick today.	i. Mona returned David's ring.
e. Ed and Carol have a test tomorrow.	j. Cindy is carrying a small suitcase.

 6 Write the correct question words in the blanks. Then complete the answers.

1. **A:** _____ is Alfredo going to go on Wednesday?

   B: He _____ to the theater.

2. **A:** _____ are you going to wear to your job interview?

   B: I _____ my new skirt.

3. **A:** _____ is going to teach your mother to use the Internet?

    B: I _____ .

4. **A:** _____ are you going to call the newspaper?

    B: _____ because I have a news story.

5. **A:** _____ are you going to make your predictions for the new year?

    B: I _____ on January 1st.

 7 **Express Yourself** A fortune-teller is a person who makes predictions about the future. Work with a partner. You are the fortune-teller. Your partner asks you to make some predictions. Ask and answer questions about money, travel, jobs, health, family, and friends. Take turns.

Example:

TRISH:	Where am I going to live in four years?
FORTUNE-TELLER:	In four years, you are going to live in New York City.
TRISH:	Am I going to work in New York?
FORTUNE-TELLER:	No, you aren't. You're going to study there.

LISTENING and SPEAKING

 1 **Before You Listen** Do you listen to weather reports? Where can you get a weather report? What does a weather report tell you?

"Today's weather is going to be … "

🎧 **②** Listen to the weather report. Complete the chart. Check your answers.

	Friday	Saturday	Sunday
Los Angeles	morning:	morning:	morning:
	afternoon:	afternoon:	afternoon:
	evening:	evening:	evening:
Mountains		morning:	morning:
		afternoon:	afternoon:
		evening:	evening:

Pronunciation

🎧 **③** Listen and repeat.

> **/y/ and /j/**
>
> **y**ellow   **J**ell-O   **y**et   **j**et

🎧 **④** Listen to each word. Circle the correct sound.

1. y   j   **3.** y   j   **5.** y   j   **7.** y   j
2. y   j   **4.** y   j   **6.** y   j   **8.** y   j

🎧 **⑤** Listen to these sentences. Then practice saying them.

a. Judy buys a yellow jacket every year in June.
b. Jane and Yolanda jumped rope for a long time yesterday.
c. Yes, I know you wore jeans to your job in July.

Speak Out

STRATEGY ▶ **Talking About Periods of Time** To talk about periods of time, you can say:

> I studied **between** three **and** five o'clock yesterday.
>
> My brother is going to study **from** four **to** six o'clock tonight.

⑥ Work with a partner. You and your partner are going to meet in the city tomorrow. One person looks at Schedule A on page 115. The other looks at Schedule B on page 116. Ask and answer questions to find out when and where you are going to meet.

Example:

A: What are you going to do between nine and ten o'clock?

B: I'm going to have coffee with a friend. Are you going to have coffee with a friend, too?

A: No, I'm not. I'm going to meet a friend for breakfast from nine to nine-thirty.

Unit 11

Schedule A

9:00–9:30	meet a friend for breakfast
9:30–10:30	go to the doctor
10:30–11:00	walk around the city
11:00–12:00	go to a job interview at **WBNC** Radio
12:00–1:30	eat lunch at Alex's Restaurant
1:30–3:00	shop for some clothes
3:00–5:00	go to a concert in the park with a friend
5:00–6:00	take the **A12** bus home

READING and WRITING

Read About It

STRATEGY ❶ **Before You Read** Look at the pictures. What is the reading about? What is interesting about the pictures?

Looking into the Future

People like to think about what the future is going to be. But did you know that some people predict the future as a job? Futurists are scientists who study and predict the future. They can guess what is going to happen in the future from the information they know now. In this way, futurists can help people and businesses get ready for the future.

What do futurists say about the future? They think there are going to be big changes in people's everyday lives—and soon! For example, cars are going to drive us to places without a driver. We're going to tell the car where we want to go, and the car is going to get us there! Some futurists think we're going to talk to people on small video telephones that we can wear, like a watch. They say we're not going to use as much paper as we do today, and we're not going to need money at all—we're going to use special cards for everything we buy!

Car of the future

Botanist in a greenhouse

Some futurists predict that scientists are going to be able to make changes in the weather. And botanists are going to make new kinds of plants so there is more food for more people. And there are going to be new ways to cook food fast.

Of course, even scientists don't really know what the future is going to be. They can only guess. But wc can be sure of one thing: the future is going to be very different, and futurists can help us get ready.

2 Read the article. Circle **T** for True or **F** for False.

    a. Futurists are scientists.   **T F**

    b. Information about the future is important for business.   **T F**

    c. People are going to wear small TVs, like a watch.   **T F**

    d. We're going to need more paper money in the future.   **T F**

    e. New plants are going to be important in the future.   **T F**

    f. Futurists really know what is going to happen in the future. **T F**

Write About It

STRATEGY

3 **Before You Write** Work with a partner. Talk about what is going to happen in the future. List your ideas in the chart.

Examples:

A: In the future, computers are going to teach children at school.

B: People are going to wear paper clothes.

A: We are going to have three months of vacation a year.

```
Computers _____
Cars _____
Food _____
Money _____
Clothes _____
Jobs _____
Vacations _____
_____
```

4 **Write** Choose three predictions from your list in Exercise 3. Write a paragraph about these predictions. Use the future tense with *be going to* + verb.

5 **Check Your Writing** Work with a partner. Read your partner's predictions. Are your predictions the same? Different? Do you agree? Disagree? Correct your sentences. Write the final copy.

- Are the future tense verbs correct?
- Is the spelling correct?

Schedule B

9:00–10:00	have coffee with a friend
10:00–10:30	walk around the city
10:30–11:00	shop for a new sweater
11:00–12:00	go see a friend at **WBNC** Radio
12:00–2:00	eat lunch at Josie's Café with my brother
2:00–2:30	buy tickets for the theater
2:30–5:00	go to a movie with brother
5:00–6:00	take the A12 bus home

GETTING STARTED

Warm Up

1 You are going to go to the airport today to meet some business people. You don't know the people, but you have their descriptions. Which of these people are you going to meet? Write the letter of the person.

1. _____ Kate Jenkins is a pretty woman. She's about thirty years old. She's five feet seven inches tall. She has long, blond, straight hair. She's slim and she wears glasses.

2. _____ Andrew Todd is a young man between twenty and twenty-five years old. He's over six feet tall. He has long, curly, brown hair and brown eyes.

3. _____ Greg Harmon is a sixty-five-year-old male. He's a short, handsome man with white hair.

Did you see anyone?

2 Listen and read.

DETECTIVE ROY: Tell me what happened.

ANNA PEREZ: Well, I came home at ten o'clock, and I thought I heard something. I turned on the light, and I saw my money box there, on the chair. It was so strange! I know I put it on the table this morning. When I opened the box, I discovered that all of my money was missing. Then I called the police.

DETECTIVE ROY: Did you see anyone?

ANNA PEREZ: Yes, I saw someone climb out of the window.

DETECTIVE ROY: Did you run after the person?

ANNA PEREZ: No! I was too afraid.

DETECTIVE ROY: Can you describe the person, Ms. Perez?

ANNA PEREZ: Oh, I don't remember much about him.

DETECTIVE ROY: You said *him*. Was the person a male?

ANNA PEREZ: I think so. He had very short hair, and he wore pants and a jacket.

DETECTIVE ROY: Was he young?

ANNA PEREZ: Yes—about twenty-one or twenty-two.

DETECTIVE ROY: What color was his hair?

ANNA PEREZ: It was blond, and it was straight.

DETECTIVE ROY: How about his eyes?

ANNA PEREZ: I don't know. I didn't see much of his face.

DETECTIVE ROY: How tall was he, and how large?

ANNA PEREZ: Hmmm … He was short, about five feet five inches tall, and slim, not heavy. He climbed out that little window.

DETECTIVE ROY: Did he take any of your things?

ANNA PEREZ: No, I don't think so. Only the money is missing.

DETECTIVE ROY: Well, Ms. Perez, you remembered a lot. With these clues, we can begin to look for the suspect.

ANNA PEREZ: Good. I want you to find him soon!

3 Answer the questions.

a. What did the suspect take?

b. What time did Anna Perez hear someone?

c. Where was the money box?

d. Did Anna remember a lot about the suspect?

e. How did Anna feel?

f. Can you describe the suspect? (Describe him.)

Building Vocabulary

Opposites

4 Write the words from the box that are the opposite.

a. straight _____   e. big _____

b. ugly _____   f. male _____

c. no one _____   g. slim _____

d. old _____   h. short _____

young	tall
heavy	little
curly	female
everyone	handsome

5 **Vocabulary Check** Write the letter of the word that answers the clue.

1. _____ You turn it on or off.   a. nose
2. _____ You sit on it.   b. table
3. _____ You see with them.   c. chair
4. _____ You hear with them.   d. box
5. _____ You smell with it.   e. light
6. _____ You eat with it.   f. eyes
7. _____ You put things in it.   g. mouth
8. _____ You eat at it.   h. ears

Talk About It

6 Work with a partner. Think of someone in the class. Have your partner guess who the person is. Ask and answer yes/no questions.

Example:

A: I'm thinking of a female.   **B:** Does she have short, curly hair?

B: Is she tall?   **A:** Yes, she does.

A: Yes, she is.   **B:** Is it Samira?

B: Does she have long hair?   **A:** Yes, it is.

A: No, she doesn't.

GRAMMAR

Someone, Something, Anyone, Anything

Someone, something, anyone, and *anything* are singular. We use *someone* or *something* in affirmative statements. We use *anyone* or *anything* in negative statements.

Bob is talking to **someone** on the phone.	My sister didn't talk to **anyone**.
Something is missing.	She didn't say **anything** to him.

We use *anyone* or *anything* in questions.

> Did you see **anyone** at the window?   Does **anyone** know what happened?
>
> Did you hear **anything** last night?   Is **anything** missing?

1 Complete the sentences with *someone, something, anyone,* or *anything.*

   a. Does _____ in your class speak English?

   b. Paul bought me _____ for my birthday.

   c. Yuki didn't tell _____ her secret.

   d. Ken doesn't know _____ about the suspect.

   e. Did _____ in your family talk to Detective Adams?

   f. Did they eat _____ good for dinner last night?

   g. Is _____ missing from your house?

   h. My mother is speaking to _____ on the phone.

No one, Nothing

No one and *nothing* are negative. They are singular.

> **No one** is there.   **Nothing** is missing.
>
> There was **no one** at the park.   Jim knew **nothing** about the suspect.

note   We do not use *not* with these words.

         anyone   *anything*

Bob **didn't see** ~~no one~~ at the park.   Jim **didn't know** ~~nothing~~ about the suspect.
                  ^   ^

Everyone, Everything

We usually use *everyone* and *everything* in affirmative statements and questions. They are also singular.

> **Everyone** in my family was there.   Is **everything** OK?

2 Complete the conversations with *no one, nothing, everyone,* or *everything.*

   1. A: Does anyone in your class have blond hair?

      B: No, _____ in our class has blond hair.

   2. A: Does anyone is your class speak English?

      B: Of course! _____ in our class speaks English.

   3. A: Did you answer the question in history class yesterday?

      B: No. I said _____ .

   4. A: Did you buy anything at the store today?

      B: Yes, I bought _____ I need.

Adjective Review

We use adjectives to describe people, places, or things. Adjectives come before nouns or after the verb *be*.

> Sharif is **young**. He has **black** hair. It's **short** and **curly**.
>
> New York City is a **big** city. It has many **famous** places.
>
> Kim has a **new** table and chair for homework. They're **brown**.

3 Look at the picture. The man with the briefcase took a small computer from an office. Work with a partner. One of you is a detective. The other one saw him leave the office. Ask and answer the questions.

Example:

A: What do you know about this man? Was he tall?

B: Yes, he was tall and thin. And he had a big briefcase.

A: What color was it?

a. Was he short or tall?
b. Was he heavy or slim?
c. Can you describe the man's hair and face?
d. What color was his jacket? his pants? his shirt? his shoes?
e. Was the briefcase big or little? What color was it?

Verb Review

Present Progressive	**Are** you **writing** to Andy?
Simple Past	No, I **wrote** to him yesterday.
Simple Present	But you **write** to him every day.
Infinitive	I know, but my father wants me **to study** today.
Future	I'**m going to write** to Andy tomorrow.

4 Complete the paragraph with the correct forms of the verbs.

Anna Perez **(1. be)** _____ nervous last night, but tonight she isn't going to worry. Detective Roy **(2. be)** _____ at her house now. He **(3. tell)** _____ her about the suspect. The detective **(4. find)** _____ the man yesterday. How did the detective find him? He **(5. describe)** _____ the suspect to Anna's neighbors. One neighbor **(6. know)** _____ the suspect. The detective asked the neighbor **(7. drive)** _____ him to the man's house. Then Detective Roy **(8. take)** _____ the suspect to the police station. Anna **(9. feel,** *neg.***)** _____ worried now.

5 Read the questions. Write the letters of the answers on the lines.
Watch the pronouns and verb tenses.

1. _____ Were the chairs next to the table?
2. _____ Is Ed handsome?
3. _____ Is Petra going to sing?
4. _____ Were you on the Internet?
5. _____ Are they sleeping?
6. _____ Is Alonzo's hair curly?
7. _____ Was there anyone in the building?
8. _____ Are you going to visit us?
9. _____ Was the baby little?
10. _____ Is there a reporter in the room?

a. No, she isn't.
b. Yes, they are.
c. No, they weren't.
d. Yes, he is.
e. Yes, there is.
f. No, it isn't.
g. Yes, she was.
h. Yes, we are.
i. No, I wasn't.
j. No, there wasn't.

6 **Express Yourself** Work with a partner. One person looks at Room A. The other person looks at Room B on p. 126. There are seven differences. Ask and answer questions to find the differences. Use *something, anything, everything, nothing, someone,* or *no one.*

Room A

Example:

A: Is anything on the TV?

B: No, there's nothing on the TV. How about in your picture? Is there anything on your TV?

A: Yes, there is. There's a picture.

LISTENING and SPEAKING

Listen: What Do You Think Is Happening?

STRATEGY **1** **Before You Listen** In a mystery story, the writer does not explain everything until the end. Do you watch mystery programs on TV? Do you read mystery stories or listen to them on audiocassettes? Why or why not?

2 Listen to the story. Answer the questions for each section after you hear it. Circle **T** for True or **F** for False.

1.
a. Two people are getting   T   F
   out of a car.
b. The people are nervous.   T   F

2.
a. Greg opened the door.   T   F
b. Carol and Greg are at   T   F
   the store.

3.
a. Sam and Paula live in   T   F
   the house.
b. Sam hears something.   T   F

4.
a. Greg is Sam's brother.   T   F
b. Sam's wife was afraid.   T   F

Pronunciation

 3 Listen and repeat.

S– Blends						
/st/	**/sp/**	**/sl/**	**/sw/**	**/sk/**	**/sn/**	**/sm/**
stand	Spain	sleeve	sweater	skirt	snack	small
stop	Spanish	sleep	swim	school	snow	smile
stone	speak	slept	swam	skin	sneeze	smell

4 Listen to the sentences. Then say them.

a. The six suspects stopped to eat snacks and sleep.

b. Mr. Smith swam at State School last Sunday.

c. Some spies are speaking Spanish to Miss Sloan.

d. Steve bought a sweater with short sleeves at the store.

Speak Out

STRATEGY **Asking Someone to Describe Him- or Herself** To ask someone to describe him- or herself, you can say:

> What do you look like?
>
> How will I recognize you?

5 You are going to the airport to meet your pen pal for the first time.

Work with a partner. Call your pen pal on the phone. Describe yourself. Take turns. What do you look like? Are you tall or short? slim or heavy? What are you going to wear?

Example:

A: Hello. Is (Masao) there?

B: Yes, this is (Masao). Who's this?

A: It's (Flora), your pen pal.

B: Oh, hi, (Flora)! How are you?

A: I'm fine, thanks. I can't wait to see you.

B: Are you going to meet me at the airport Saturday?

A: Yes, I am. How will I recognize you? What do you look like?

B: Well, I'm tall and slim. I have straight black hair, and I wear glasses. I'm going to wear a short, blue jacket and jeans. I have a brown backpack. How will I recognize you?

Read About It

STRATEGY ▶ **1** **Before You Read** Look at the floor plan below. What do you see? Describe the room. Look at the pictures. What do you think the mystery is about?

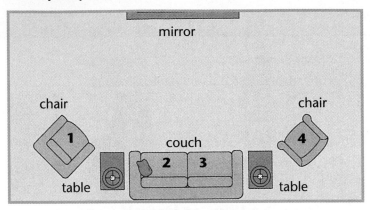

Mr. Smith's Living Room

2 A good mystery writer makes the reader think that everyone is a suspect. Read the mystery. One man in the room is a spy. The spy is going to put poison in another man's drink. Who is the spy? Who is going to have the poison in his drink?

Who Did It?

Four men are sitting in a room. Two men are sitting on a couch, and one is sitting in each chair. The men's last names are Smith, Brown, Robinson, and Osborn. One is a teacher, one is an actor, one is a pilot, and one is a doctor.

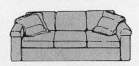

couch

a. Mr. Smith's daughter takes a soft drink to Robinson, some tea to Osborn, and some coffee to Brown.

b. The actor looks in the mirror and sees the door close behind Smith's daughter.

c. Osborn is sitting to the right of the actor.

d. The doctor is sitting in a chair on Brown's left.

e. Smith, Osborn, and Brown don't have sisters.

f. The doctor doesn't have anything to drink.

g. The pilot's brother-in-law is the actor. He is sitting next to Osborn.

h. The pilot is sitting in a chair.

i. The pilot and the teacher put their drinks on the same table.

j. Someone put poison in a cup of tea.

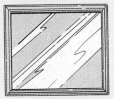

mirror

cup

Work with a partner. You are detectives. Your job is to stop the spy! Read the clues and look at the floor plan on page 124. Answer the questions and complete the chart.

1. Look at clues **a** and **f**. Who is the doctor?   _____
2. Look at clues **e** and **g**. Who is the pilot?   _____
3. Look at clues **d** and **h**. Who are sitting on chairs?   _____
4. Look at clues **b**, **c**, and **g**. Who is on the couch on the left? _____
5. Look at clues **c** and **g**. Who is on the couch on the right?   _____
6. Look at clues **b** and **g**. Who is the actor?   _____
7. Look at clues **c** and **i**. What is Osborn's occupation?   _____

People	Drinks	Occupations	Chair 1	Couch 2	Couch 3	Chair 4
Smith						
Brown						
Robinson						
Osborn						

Write About It

STRATEGY ④ **Before You Write** You are going to write a mystery story. Look at the picture clues. Make notes on page 126. Write one or two sentences to describe each picture.

a.

b.

c.

d.

e.

f.

Your Notes from the Picture Clues

Example:

Four people are in a car. One person is driving. Three people are sleeping.

a. _____

_____

b. _____

_____

c. _____

_____

d. _____

_____

e. _____

_____

f. _____

_____

⑤ Write Use your notes to write your mystery story.

☑ **⑥ Check Your Writing** Work with a partner. Read each other's stories. Correct your sentences if necessary. Write the final copy.

- Is the story a mystery? Is the reader going to understand what happened?
- Are the verb tenses correct?
- Are the adjectives correct?

Room B

1 Complete the sentences with the correct form of *be going to*.

I **(1. exercise,** *neg.***)** _____ tonight. I
(2. exercise) _____ tomorrow. Tonight we
(3. do) _____ something fun.

Paulo **(4. go,** *neg.***)** _____ to work today. What
(5. he, do) _____? I think he **(6. take)** _____
his daughter to her new school.

What **(7. Judy, do)** _____ next week?
She **(8. drive)** _____ a car to school.
(9. she, drive) _____ alone? No!
She **(10. drive)** _____ with her driving teacher, of course!

2 Write statements or questions.

1. to/Harry's/Internet/taught/the/use/grandson/him

_____.

2. me/this/do/letter/What/want/to/with/you/do

_____?

3. is/Mr./on/vacation/week/going/Henderson/to/go/next

_____.

4. to/easy/Silvio/an/English/me/find/him/for/book/asked

_____.

5. ring/bought/Jim/a/beautiful/Elizabeth/for

_____.

3 Answer the questions. Write two sentences for each question.

1. What do you do every day?

_____.
_____.

2. What did you do yesterday?

_____.
_____.

3. What are you going to do tomorrow?

_____.
_____.

4. What important things did you learn when you were young?

_____.
_____.

5. What are you afraid of? Why?

_____.
_____.

4 Complete the conversation. Use *someone, anyone, everyone,* or *no one;* or *something, anything, everything,* or *nothing.*

DETECTIVE: Is this your car, sir?

PETER: Yes. **(1.)** _____ knows it's my car. Is **(2.)** _____ wrong?

DETECTIVE: I don't know. **(3.)** _____ called me because the car door was open. Please look inside the car. Is **(4.)** _____ missing?

PETER: Hmm. No, **(5.)** _____ is missing. **(6.)** _____ is here.

DETECTIVE: Good. Then **(7.)** _____ is OK.

PETER: But this is so strange! Did **(8.)** _____ see what happened?

DETECTIVE: No, **(9.)** _____ saw **(10.)** _____ next to your car.

PETER: Wait! I think **(11.)** _____ is missing!

DETECTIVE: What is it?

PETER: My watch! **(12.)** _____ took my watch!

Vocabulary Review

Complete the sentences with words or phrases from the box.

interview	female
snowy	light
around	soon
under	different from
area code	make a mistake

1. Do you want to take a taxi or a bus _____ the city?

2. I waited two hours for the _____, because I really wanted the job.

3. British English is _____ American English.

4. My mother was the first _____ detective in the city police.

5. Did you see the weather report? Tomorrow is going to be cold and _____.

6. Ted did his homework on the computer. It was long, but he didn't _____!

7. Please write your _____ and telephone number.

8. You can find a computer school in the telephone book _____ "Freida's Schools."

9. Please turn off the _____. I need to sleep.

10. It's spring! _____ the weather is going to be sunny and hot.

Base Form	Simple Past	Base Form	Simple Past
be: am, is, are	was, were	put	put
build	built	read	read
buy	bought	ride	rode
come	came	run	ran
do	did	say	said
drink	drank	see	saw
drive	drove	sing	sang
eat	atc	sit	sat
find	found	sleep	slept
fly	flew	speak	spoke
get	got	stand	stood
go	went	swim	swam
have, has	had	take	took
hear	heard	tell	told
know	knew	think	thought
lose	lost	understand	understood
make	made	wear	wore
mean	meant	win	won
meet	met	write	wrote

THE INTERNATIONAL PHONETIC ALPHABET

Consonants

/b/	**b**a**b**y, clu**b**	/n/	**n**o, opi**n**ion	/ð/	**th**is, mo**th**er, ba**the**
/d/	**d**own, to**d**ay, sa**d**	/ŋ/	a**ng**ry, lo**ng**	/v/	**v**ery, tra**v**el, o**f**
/f/	**f**un, pre**f**er, laugh	/p/	**p**a**p**er, ma**p**	/w/	**w**ay, any**o**ne
/g/	**g**ood, be**g**in, do**g**	/r/	**r**ain, pa**r**ent, doo**r**	/y/	**y**es, on**i**on
/h/	**h**ome, be**h**ind	/s/	**s**alt, medi**c**ine, bu**s**	/z/	**z**oo, cou**s**in, alway**s**
/k/	**k**ey, cho**c**olate, bla**ck**	/š/	**s**ugar, spe**ci**al, fi**sh**	/ž/	mea**s**ure, gara**g**e
/l/	**l**ate, po**l**ice, mai**l**	/t/	**t**ea, ma**t**erial, da**t**e	/č/	**ch**eck, pi**c**ture, wat**ch**
/m/	**m**ay, wo**m**an, swi**m**	/θ/	**th**ing, heal**th**y, ba**th**	/ǰ/	**j**ob, refri**g**erator, oran**g**e

Vowels

/a/	**o**n, h**o**t, f**a**ther	/e/	**A**pril, tr**ai**n, s**ay**	/ɪ/	p**u**t, c**oo**k, w**ou**ld
/æ/	**a**nd, c**a**sh	/i/	**e**ven, sp**ea**k, tr**ee**	/ə/	**a**bout, penc**i**l, lem**o**n
/ɛ/	**e**gg, s**ay**s, l**ea**ther	/o/	**o**pen, cl**o**se, sh**ow**	/ɚ/	m**o**ther, Satur**d**ay, doct**or**
/ɪ/	**i**n, b**i**g	/u/	b**oo**t, d**o**, thr**ough**	/ɝ/	**ear**th, b**ur**n, h**er**
/ɔ/	**o**ff, d**au**ghter, dr**aw**	/ʌ/	**o**f, y**ou**ng, s**u**n		

Diphthongs

/aɪ/	**i**ce, st**y**le, l**ie**	/au/	**ou**t, d**ow**n, h**ow**	/ɔɪ/	**oi**l, n**oi**se, b**oy**

THE ENGLISH ALPHABET

Here is the pronunciation of the letters of the English alphabet, written in International Phonetic Alphabet symbols.

a	/e/	h	/eč/	o	/o/	v	/vi/
b	/bi/	i	/aɪ/	p	/pi/	w	/ˈdʌbəlˌyu/
c	/si/	j	/ǰe/	q	/kyu/	x	/ɛks/
d	/di/	k	/ke/	r	/ar/	y	/waɪ/
e	/i/	l	/ɛl/	s	/ɛs/	z	/zi/
f	/ɛf/	m	/ɛm/	t	/ti/		
g	/ǰi/	n	/ɛn/	u	/yu/		

UNIT VOCABULARY

STARTING OUT

Articles
a
an

Nouns
a backpack
a book
a briefcase
a bus
a car
chalk
chalkboard
a computer
a desk

a door
an eraser
paper
a pen
a pencil
a plane
a window

Things to Do
Answer a question.
Ask a question.
Listen.
Look at picture 1.
Raise your hand.

Repeat.
Sit down.
Stand up.

Things to Say
Can you help me,
  please?
I don't know.
I don't understand.
Of course.
What's this?
Work with a partner.

Titles
Mr.
Ms.

Expressions
Good afternoon.
Good-bye.
Good evening.
Good morning.
Good night.
Hello.
Hi.
How are you?
See you later.

UNIT 1

Conjunction
and

Nouns
a name
a number
a pen pal
a postcard
a question
a taxi
a word

Occupations
an actor
an actress
an athlete
a dentist
a doctor
a (bus) driver
a nurse
a pilot
a secretary
a singer

a student
a teacher
a writer

Verbs
answer
ask
be: am/is/are
spell

Pronouns
I
you
she
he
it
we
they

**Possessive
Adjectives**
my
your

her
his

Wh– words
What?
Where?

Expressions
Are you ready ... ?
I'm sorry.
Nice to meet you.
What do you do?
What does he/she
  do?
Where are you from?

Numbers
one
two
three
four
five
six

seven
eight
nine
ten
eleven
twelve
thirteen
fourteen
fifteen
sixteen
seventeen
eighteen
nineteen
twenty

Other
from
no
ready
right
wrong
yes

UNIT 2

Nouns
address
business
drum
form
guitar
passport
piano
suitcase
ticket
vacation

Places
airport
city
hospital
hotel
office
school
street
theater

People
boy
clerk
flight attendant
friend
girl
man
musician
woman

Verbs
do/does
fill in/fills in
have/has
live/lives
mean/means
play/plays
speak/speaks
work/works

UNIT 2 continued

Prepositions of Place	Expressions	Here it is./Here they are.	Other
at	Excuse me.	May I have (your form)?	first
in	Have a nice (vacation).	You're welcome.	last
on			too

UNIT 3

Conjunctions	grandmother	make	fifty-four
but	grandson	read	sixty-five
or	husband	ride	seventy-six
	mother	run	eighty-seven
Nouns	sister	sing	ninety-eight
bike	son	swim	one hundred
pie	wife/wives	use (a computer)	one thousand
plant		walk	
	Verbs	write	**Other**
Family	cook		about
brother	dance	**Numbers**	can/can't
daughter	drive	twenty-one	false
father	eat	thirty-two	that
granddaughter	explain	forty-three	true
grandfather			

UNIT 4

Prepositions of Place	*Clothes*	**Verbs**	pink
across from	dress	buy	purple
between	jacket	come	red
next to	jeans	design	white
	pants	like	yellow
Nouns	shirt	sell	
advertisement	shoe	shop (for)	**Expressions**
bike	skirt	want	How about (this shirt)?
bookstore	sock	wear	on sale
day	sweater		(She's) wearing (a jacket).
mall	T-shirt	**Adjectives**	(They're) wearing (jeans).
music		large	What's (she) wearing?
plant	*Days of the Week*	long	
salesperson	Monday	nice	**Other**
shoe	Tuesday	short	any/some
sleeve	Wednesday	small	for
store	Thursday		there
video	Friday	*Colors*	these/those
week	Saturday	black	with
	Sunday	blue	without
		brown	
		green	
		orange	

UNIT 5

Nouns	*Months*	August	butter
birthday	January	September	a cake
idea	February	October	cheese
problem	March	November	chocolate
restaurant	April	December	(a cup of) coffee
today	May		an egg
year	June	*Food*	a hamburger
	July	bread	a hot dog

UNIT VOCABULARY

UNIT 5 continued

(a head of) lettuce
(a glass of) milk
an onion
(a piece of) pizza
a salad
a sandwich
sugar
a tomato

Drinks
coffee
milk
soft drink
tea

Verbs
drink
need

Adjectives
great
hungry
old
thirsty

Possessive Adjectives
its
our
their

Wh– **word**
When?

Expressions
I'd like (some cake).
Let's (go).

Other
every

UNIT 6

Prepositions of Place
behind
in front of

Nouns
camera
clock
glasses
letter
magazine
money

motorcycle
newspaper
park
story
time

People
mail carrier
neighbor
reporter
spy

Verbs
carry
follow
get
get off/on
happen
stop
take a picture
think
wait (for)

Adjectives
new
strange

Wh– **word**
Who?

Expressions
How (strange)!
It's (three) o'clock.
What time is it?

Other
now

UNIT 7

Nouns
ad
basketball
club
homework
house
juice
member
pool
room
tonight

TV
water

Meals
breakfast
lunch
dinner
a snack

Fruit
apple
grape
orange

Verbs
exercise
jump (rope)
know how
lift (weights)
see
watch

Adjectives
easy
fun
hard
healthy

Expressions
How often… ?
Me, neither!
Me, too.
What kind of … ?

Other
a lot of
also
in/out of shape

UNIT 8

Conjunction
because

Nouns
hour
minute
ring
soap opera

Verbs
be: was/were
call
cry
love

return
say

Object Pronouns
him
me
them
us

Adjectives
Feelings
afraid
angry
confused

happy
nervous
sad
shocked
sick
tired
terrible
tired
worried

Wh– **words**
Why?
How long?

Time Expressions
last (year)
then
yesterday

Expressions
How do you feel?
I can't stand it!

Other
alone
another
favorite
in love
not

UNIT 9

Nouns
building
calendar
date
history
moon
mountain
ruins
star
stone
sun
test
war

Regular Past Tense Verbs
climb/climbed
discover/discovered
learn/learned
look for/looked for
remember/ remembered
study/studied

Irregular Past Tense Verbs
build/built
buy/bought
come/came

do/did
eat/ate
find/found
get/got back
go/went
have/had
lose/lost
make/made
read/read
ride/rode
see/saw
speak/spoke
swim/swam
take/took

think/thought
win/won
write/wrote

Adjectives
famous
real
second
third

Expressions
When (were) (you) born?
Why don't you (start)?

UNIT 10

Nouns
adult
article
baby
child/children
design
information
interview
job
neighborhood
the news

opinion
radio
report
reporter
sale
telephone/phone
weekend

Verbs
agree
clean
disagree

find out/found out
make a mistake
tell/told

Adjectives
bid
clean
dirty
fat
free
pretty
tall

thin
ugly

Expressions
All right.
Would you like … ?

Other
early
late
more

UNIT 11

Prepositions of Direction
around
down
over
under
up

Nouns
future
horoscope

past
prediction
scientist

Verbs
(be) going to
believe
get/got married
guess
predict

Adjectives
Weather
cloudy
cold
hot
rainy/rain
snowy/snow
sunny
windy

Expressions
That's amazing!
What's new?
What's the weather like?

Other
different
the same (as)
soon
tomorrow

UNIT 12

Nouns
box
chair
clue
description
light
table

People
detective
female/male
police/police officer
suspect

Body
ear
eye
face
hair
mouth
nose

Verbs
describe
hear/heard
put/put
turn off (on)

Adjectives
blond
curly
handsome
heavy
missing
slim
straight
young

Expressions
I think so./I don't think so.

Measurements
foot/feet
inch/inches

Other
anyone
anything
everyone
everything
no one
nothing
someone
something

INDEX

Numbers indicate units. (SO = Starting Out)